Endorsements

"Robyn Gool, an honored graduate of Oral Roberts University and a star tennis player on our athletic program, who heeded God's call to preach the Gospel, is one of the ablest, most dedicated, and anointed young pastors in America. I believe in him, affirm him, and recommend his new book, *What to Do When You're Backed against the Wall,* without reservation. It is a winner. And it could very well change your life by positively affecting every area of your being, as it has mine."

—Oral Roberts, Founder and Chancellor,
Oral Roberts University

"I have reviewed Pastor Gool's book and feel this is a very pertinent book; his points are right in line with God's Word. These are breakthroughs we can never read or hear too much about because we can often lose the battle in our minds. I believe this book can bring a breakthrough when you are against the wall. Pastor Gool is a man who believes what he is writing, and it works and works and works! I know I have to constantly pull down negative strongholds and replace them with positive strength found in God's Word. I highly recommend this book."

—Marilyn Hickey
Bible teacher, Marilyn Hickey Ministries

"Pastor Robyn Gool provides the most practical, inspirational, and uplifting direction to anyone with his back to the wall. This great book is full of faith, spiritual wisdom, and encouragement from one of the most encouraging pastors I have met. If you become a doer of the fabulous fifteen points outlined in this positive, enthusiastic work, you will face your mountains with the tools to overcome and walk out the victory God has prepared for you. Read it, apply it, and you'll know *What to Do When You're Backed against the Wall.*"
—Tommy Barnett, Pastor, Phoenix First Assembly

"*What to Do When You're Backed against the Wall* hits the nail on the head. When I first read it, I wanted to shout 'bull's eye.' Without question, the mind is the battlefield. Satan, the Serpent, would never have succeeded with Eve had he not gotten into her mind. Pastor Gool is absolutely on target when he proclaims, 'You must take charge of your thoughts and gird your mind.' This is a book for all to read. Everyone at some time has had his or her back against the wall. The sound biblical instructions found in this book will turn you around and cause Satan to find his back against the wall of faith and God's Word. I am thankful for pastors like Robyn Gool whom the Lord is using to cause people to live a victorious life in Christ. Once you have fully spiritually digested the truth in this book, pass it on. There are many people around you who have their backs against a wall."
—Hilton Sutton, Th.D.
Chairman, Hilton Sutton World Ministries

What to Do When

YOU'RE

Backed

AGAINST

the

WALL

What to Do When

YOU'RE

Backed

AGAINST

the

WALL

Robyn Gool

WHAT TO DO WHEN YOU'RE BACKED AGAINST THE WALL

To contact the author:
Victory Christian Center
P.O. Box 240433
Charlotte, NC 28224

ISBN: 0-88368-654-6
Printed in the United States of America
© 2000 by Robyn Gool

Whitaker House
30 Hunt Valley Circle
New Kensington, PA 15068

Library of Congress Cataloging-in-Publication Data

Gool, Robyn, 1953–
    What to do when you're backed against the wall / Robyn Gool.
        p.   cm.
    ISBN 0-88368-654-6 (alk. paper)
    1. Christian life. I. Title.
    BV4501.3 .G66 2001
    248.8'6—dc21
                                                    00-012781

1 2 3 4 5 6 7 8 9 10 11 12 / 08 07 06 05 04 03 02 01

Contents

Foreword

Once again, Robyn Gool has hit a home run in this book of outstanding teaching from the Word of God concerning what to do when you're backed against the wall.

Robyn is giving hard-hitting, no-nonsense, straight-ahead teaching, just the way I like it. He explains how to take the Word of God and win over any situation that attacks believers everywhere and tries to get their backs against the wall.

It has been my privilege to know Robyn Gool and his family and ministry for almost twenty years. We have ministered together in the USA and overseas, and I've watched his children (two of whom have been overseas with me) grow into fine young adults. Jackie and I truly count the Gool family as our own.

I have recommended Robyn and Marilyn constantly to people both at home and abroad, so it's certainly no problem to recommend this book to you to read and read again. I urge you to apply the Word-based principles herein to your life to be the winner God designed you to be.

When you're backed against the wall, the only way out is up. God has your answer; the steps are laid out in this book. Remember, God sees you as more than a conqueror. So does Robyn Gool, and so do I. God bless you.

For the world that cost the blood of Jesus!
— Terry L. Mize, International missionary and author of *More Than Conquerors*

Chapter 1

Guard Your Mind

When you're backed against the wall, the very first thing you must do is to guard and take control of your mind. The mind is the battleground of life. Whether you win or lose depends on your ability to govern your thoughts. If you allow your thinking to run rampant, replaying one negative thought after another, you will lose the battle for your mind.

Take Control of Your Mind

Again, the first thing to do is to capture the thoughts of your mind. Control them. Don't let them run wild. Refuse to allow your mind to race a hundred miles a minute. During stressful situations, your mind wants to focus on negative, destructive thoughts. Such thoughts will pressure you to give up or to compromise your integrity. That's when you must command your mind to "shut up." You must take control of your mind: *"As [a man] thinketh in his heart, so is he"* (Proverbs 23:7).

Negative thoughts will only cloud your thinking and prevent you from discerning which thoughts are of God and which ones aren't.

God teaches us in His Word to control our minds and not allow them to control us. Mental institutions and psychiatric wards are full of people whose negative thoughts gained control of their minds and eventually drove them insane. Many complained of being tormented by voices, long before they were institutionalized. Rather than being audible, distinguishable sounds, these voices first surfaced in their minds as compelling thoughts.

Regaining control of your mind will come from reading, meditating on, and confessing God's Word, and praying in the spirit. But you must first distinguish between God-sent, faith-driven thoughts and Satan-inspired fears.

Even Christians, when they're not prayerful, can be deceived by Satan's tactics. The Bible says the Devil can transform himself into *"an angel of light"* (2 Corinthians 11:14), making himself appear to be God. The Devil will subtly plant a seemingly good thought into a Christian's mind like: "Read your Bible all day. Read your Bible all the time."

To most of us, that would appear to be a thought from the Holy Spirit. Consequently, we get out of bed feeling compelled to read our Bibles all day. When it's time to go to work, the thought becomes even stronger: "No, keep on reading. I want to show you something this morning."

By now we're thinking, "This must be God," and we continue reading until we're late for work. We get another thought, convincing us to stay home and continue reading. After we've missed work and skipped breakfast, lunch, and dinner to

10

continue reading, the Devil convinces us to read all through the night.

My friend, compulsive and obsessive thoughts are of the Devil. I know Christians who have literally heard voices telling them to read all the time or to pray constantly. If they didn't follow these directives, they felt guilty and heavily condemned. Guilt and condemnation are not from God. That's bondage!

Many times, Christians follow whims, not knowing if their thoughts are from God or the Devil. Whenever you are *driven* to do something, even a seemingly good thing, usually those thoughts are of the Devil. Devilish compulsions cause people not to eat or sleep properly, to neglect their responsibilities, and to become obsessed with doing good deeds.

Watch out for all kinds of compulsive thoughts that urge you to do things constantly, like missing work in order to read the Bible or to witness all the time, which could result in your losing your job. I encourage Christians who complain about not having enough time to spend with God because of their jobs or college classes to keep their jobs and remain in school. The Bible says that if a man doesn't work, he shouldn't be allowed to eat. (See 2 Thessalonians 3:10.)

Likewise, God has commanded you to take care of your body. Jesus took His disciples away from the crowds to rest at times. God knows that you need rest and proper nourishment to stay healthy and strong. Otherwise, you will open the door for the Devil to put sickness and disease on you. The thoughts driving some to become

workaholics are as detrimental as thoughts compelling others never to work.

Know the Voice of God

So how do you learn to tell where your
thoughts originate? You must recognize the voice
of God and understand what the Bible says your
thoughts should be. Paul wrote,

> *Finally, brethren, whatsoever things are true,*
> *whatsoever things are honest, whatsoever*
> *things are just, whatsoever things are pure,*
> *whatsoever things are lovely, whatsoever*
> *things are of good report; if there be any*
> *virtue, and if there be any praise, think on*
> *these things.*   (Philippians 4:8)

God wants you to finish your education, work
productively on your job, and shine as the light of
the world. He expects you to be an example to the
lost by witnessing to them, living holy, confessing
what He says, and seizing every opportunity to
lead them to Jesus. If God pulls all of His people
out of the world to live like cloistered monks,
reading the Bible and praying all day, how will
the world be saved?

God can magnify the fifteen minutes you
spend with Him, making it richer than eight hours
spent by someone who views spending time with
God as a religious chore.

Meditate on the verses you have time to read,
and God will make them potent, powerful, rich,
and full of revelation. As you meditate on the
Word, God will reveal to you how to stop harmful,

negative thoughts that may be lodged in your mind and how to counter the Devil's onslaught of new ones.

Pull Down Negative Strongholds

Second Corinthians 10:4–5 says,

(For the weapons of our warfare are not carnal, but mighty through God to the pulling down of strong holds;) casting down imaginations, and every high thing that exalteth itself against the knowledge of God, and bringing into captivity every thought to the obedience of Christ.

The Bible teaches us to pull down strongholds and cast down imaginations. One dictionary defines *stronghold* as "a place having strong defenses—a fortified place." All strongholds begin in the mind. If you entertain any thought long enough, whether it is good or bad, it becomes established in your thinking.

Suicidal tendencies are caused by satanic strongholds. Yet not all strongholds are negative. For the person who has made an unwavering commitment to tithe, tithing has become a stronghold—a fortress in his mind. Tithing is a positive stronghold. Because the tither automatically writes out his tithe check when he gets paid, the Devil has a tough time implanting thoughts to rob God of His tithes.

So there are positive and negative strongholds. But when you're backed against the wall, and all kinds of negative thoughts bombard you,

you have to take control of your mind so that Satan cannot use it to establish a negative stronghold.

When you're backed against the wall, your imagination will magnify your fears. The person who has just lost a job begins to think: "I guess I'm going to lose my car and my house. I will not be able to pay my bills. My lights and gas will be cut off, and I'll soon be sleeping on the streets."

Negative imaginations are fueled by fear. You have to cast them down because no one else can do that for you. Paul described imaginations as *"every high thing that exalteth itself against the knowledge of God"* (2 Corinthians 10:5). That includes philosophies, secular and religious thinking, and everything that isn't biblically sound.

Paul also told us to bring *"into captivity every thought to the obedience of Christ"* (v. 5). Thoughts that do not line up with God's Word must be cast down. When you're backed against the wall, you must immediately control your thoughts.

You must say, "No, this is not of God, and I will not think on it! I will not think about going under. I'm going over."

Be Practical

God made us to be lights, not show-offs. He did not intend for us to be exhibitionists, attracting attention by showboating all the time. Our conduct should be normal, yet different in that we're peaceable, prosperous, and joyful in the midst of the world's turmoil and strife.

If thoughts come to you encouraging you to be different so that you can make a name for yourself, those thoughts are originating with the Enemy. If you don't recognize that, you will wind up acting strangely, and people will not want to associate with you. But you'll mistake their disassociation as jealousy of your calling or office. You will have been deceived by the voices you have listened to and the thoughts that you have entertained.

Jesus was a prophet and intercessor, yet He socialized and mingled with people in a normal way. Apart from spending a lengthy time in the wilderness praying and fasting, prior to beginning His public ministry (see Matthew 4:1–11), Jesus did not spend an inordinate amount of time praying alone. Of course, He was in constant communion with the Father, but He did not retreat into a life of prayer and thus neglect doing the Father's will. There were times during the day when He went to a mountain and prayed (Matthew 14:23; Mark 6:46; Luke 9:28). We also read that He prayed all night before choosing His disciples (Luke 6:12), but, primarily, He went about doing His Father's business all day, while still finding time to pray.

For most people, doing their Father's business will be exemplifying God's light in the workplace. God expects Christians to work hard, support their families, and spend quality time at home ministering to their families properly. Usually, thoughts contrary to that are not of God.

If you do not discern your thoughts, pull down strongholds, and cast down imaginations, then your behavior, conversation, and appearance will become weird. The Devil will have you doing impulsive things. At some point, you may have to seek Christian counseling to help you regain control of your mind. Otherwise, you may have to turn to hospitals and medication for treatment.

The Devil comes to steal, kill, and destroy (John 10:10). It doesn't matter to him how he does it. He loves to make Jesus look bad through His people. I remember a Christian standing on a corner at a main intersection, spinning around at intervals because he believed God had told him to do so. Of course, this made God look bad, especially when the man was taken to the hospital proclaiming that God had told him to do it. The Devil loves to make God's people look foolish. It's a way of getting back at God.

If he can get you to lose your job because you are at home every day reading your Bible, that makes Jesus look bad. If he can get you to give all your money away, so that your bills go unpaid or you're facing bankruptcy, that makes Jesus look bad. If he can get you to buy teaching tapes, good books, groceries, or things your children need, instead of paying your bills, that makes Jesus look bad.

God is a practical God—an everyday kind of God. He doesn't want us looking weird and doing stupid, foolish things. We must guard our minds in order to make the right decisions at the right time.

When you're backed against the wall—

Guard your mind.

Chapter 2

Get Specific Instructions

Quieting your mind is as important as taking control of your mind. It is important because you need to find out if God has any information or special instructions for you. Simply pray and ask Him what to do about any situation. Then ask Him to give you guidelines or directives for overcoming it. Your prayer could be as simple as, "God, is there anything You want me to know right now?" This prayer acknowledges His Lordship in the situation.

In 2 Kings 3, the Israelites found their backs against the wall as they united with Judah and Edom to fight against the Moabites. Soon they realized they had exhausted their water supply and had no access to more. So the kings called for Elisha, the man of God, who gave them specific instructions on how to get water. However, Elisha's instructions seemed anything but logical.

In this arid desert land without rain or wind, Elijah told them that the Lord said to dig a valley full of ditches, and that without their seeing or hearing wind or rain, God would fill them with water. That's exactly what happened. Not only did the children of Israel have plenty of water to drink, but the Lord also confounded the Moabites, causing them to suffer great defeat and to retreat from the battle.

Don't expect God to tell you when to go to eat, where to shop, or what to wear every day. However, when you're faced with a crisis, see if He has information for you that you don't already know. His instructions can seem odd, but they always lead to victory.

God does talk to us. Obviously, God will not tell you every little thing to do. He does not control you or make decisions for you. In a crisis, He may or may not say anything. If He does tell you something, obey! If He doesn't, rely on your sound judgment. God's silence may be His way of reminding you that He has already shown you how to handle the situation.

He expects you to walk in what you know rather than look for new revelation. God expects us to get answers by praying to Him, meditating on His Word, and being led by the Holy Spirit. Never press into the realm of the supernatural for answers from God. Peter wrote,

> *We have also a more sure word of prophecy; whereunto ye do well that ye take heed, as unto a light that shineth in a dark place, until the day dawn, and the day star arise in your hearts.* (2 Peter 1:19)

This Scripture means that the Word of God is surer than angelic visitations, visions, or signs. If they come, they come, but they do not supersede the Word of God. If you seek supernatural voices, signs, visions, or dreams, you will probably get them. The Devil will send you a counterfeit to trick you into believing you're receiving signs from God. Always put the Word of God above any manifestations.

If you have no specific instructions from the Word or Spirit of God, then weigh the pros and cons of the situation before making your decision. Your attitude should always be: "If God is big enough to divide the Red Sea, surely He can talk to me. No good thing will He withhold from me. (See Psalm 84:11.) Since He has not given any specific instructions, there must not be anything else that I need to know or that I have left undone."

When you're backed against the wall—

See if God has specific instructions for you.

Chapter 3

Be Aggressive

When you're backed against the wall, be aggressive. Rise up like a lion and roar. Aggressive people run out of the starting gate ready to win. When you're passive, you're laid back, taking no action. God's people are to have the attitude: "I am coming out of this mess. I am going forward, and I won't take no for an answer." They are to be as Balaam prophesied:

> Behold, the people shall rise up as a great lion, and lift up himself as a young lion; he shall not lie down until he eat of the prey, and drink the blood of the slain. (Numbers 23:24)

When you're backed against the wall, remember: you can't back up any further anyway. That's when you've got to charge forward, saying, "I am coming after you, Goliath. I am coming after you, problem. I am coming after you, Satan." Get aggressive, rise up like a lion, and don't lie down until you have "eaten your prey."

Go on the Offensive

Every time our church encountered problems in building our multi-purpose facility, I went on the offensive. When the city inspectors and project manager told us we couldn't move in by our deadline, I said, "If I have to go over your head, we're going to be in there by our deadline." They said, "Oh, no, you won't. There is no way, Rev. Gool." But I insisted there was a way, and there was. I went to the mayor, who got us all the permits we needed, allowing us to meet our deadline.

When you're backed against the wall, you must become aggressive. There are too many cowards in the camp today—too many weak-kneed Christians with no backbone, determination, or courage.

Apparently, those inspectors had been influenced by the Devil because all our building plans and specifications were in order. Our contractors and project manager had assured us that everything was completed, and there was no reason for our opening to be delayed. My back was against the wall, and I knew it was time to be aggressive. I was not going to let the Devil run my life.

Go Forward

When you're backed against the wall, you can't afford to quit, sit down, put your feet up, or watch television all night. That's when you've got to get up and tell the Devil you are not going to sleep yet. Tell him you are getting ready to cause an ambushment in the realm of the spirit, and you're getting ready to bring confusion to him and his cohorts. You do this by praise, praying in tongues, confessing the promises of God, and taking authority over the Devil.

When all hell breaks loose, go forward. I don't care what the storm is like; you can lick it in the name of Jesus Christ of Nazareth. Jesus said the gates of hell will not prevail against His church (Matthew 16:18). James said to submit yourself to God, resist the Devil, *"and he will flee from you"* (James 4:7).

We have armor that includes a shield of faith. (See Ephesians 6:11–17.) Put your shield of faith out there and quench all the *"fiery darts"* (v. 16) of the Wicked One. If the doctors tell you that you are going to die, get aggressive. Listen to more tapes, spend more time meditating on the Word of God, pray in tongues more, and act as if you are healed.

If you're able to get out of bed, do it. Get up every morning, dress, and act healed to the best of your ability. If there is pain in your body, say out loud, "By His stripes, I am healed!" (See 1 Peter 2:24.)

Show the Devil that he is a liar and that Jesus is your Lord. The Bible says that David *"ran toward the army to meet the Philistine"* Goliath (1 Samuel 17:48). Your problem is not going to disappear. You have to make things happen. We are in covenant with God, who said that when our enemies come against us one way, they will flee before us *"seven ways"* (Deuteronomy 28:7).

When you're backed against the wall—

Be aggressive.

Chapter 4

Remind God of His Word

The fourth thing we can do when our backs are against the wall is to remind God of His Word. Because we are in covenant with Him, there is no need to cry in despair, rely on everybody we know to pray for us, or hold a spiritual pity party.

This is the time to remind God of His Word, just as He told us to do: *"Put me in remembrance"* (Isaiah 43:26).

Flex Your Spiritual Muscles

When my back is against the wall, I don't look for sympathy. I don't look for someone to pat me on the back and say, "Oh, Lord, have mercy. I'm going to pray for you! I trust things will get better."

Instead, I'm going to flex my spiritual muscles and say, "I am more than a conqueror through Him who loved me (Romans 8:37). If God is for me, who can be against me (v. 31)? *'The LORD is on my side; I will not fear'* (Psalm 118:6). If God and I are in agreement, we are the majority!"

When you're backed against the wall, you need to begin to say, "God, You said You would supply all of my needs according to Your riches in

23

glory by Christ Jesus (Philippians 4:19). God, You said You would make a way in the wilderness and rivers in the desert (Isaiah 43:19). God, You said You would go before me and make the crooked places straight (Isaiah 40:4). God, You said...." Quote all of the other promises you can remember or find in the Bible.

Know the Scriptures

When God told us to put Him in remembrance, He meant that we must approach Him and remind Him of what He has said.

Obviously, that's not because God can't remember what He said. It is to make sure that we know what He said, because He watches over His Word to perform it. We can't remind Him or anyone else of what God said, unless we know what He said. That puts the responsibility of knowing the Word of God on us.

Paul wrote to Timothy, his young disciple, concerning this responsibility. His letter was an admonition to all Christians. He said,

Study to show thyself approved unto God, a workman that needeth not to be ashamed, rightly dividing the word of truth.
(2 Timothy 2:15)

Acknowledge Your Covenant

It is our responsibility to read our Bibles and to meditate on the Word of God so that we can know for certain what our Father said He would

24

do. After all, we are in covenant with Him, and if that covenant is broken, we are the ones who break it.

Psalm 89:34 says that God will not break covenant with us. God says again in Judges 2:1 that He will never break His covenant with you.

We are in covenant with the living God, the Creator of heaven and earth, the One *"who raised Jesus from the dead"* (Romans 8:11 NKJV). And He said, *"I will never break my covenant with you"* (Judges 2:1).

Because you are in covenant with God, you have a right to declare that His wisdom is your wisdom, His ability is your ability, His resources are your resources, and His power is now your power. You must receive and claim them all in the name of Jesus. Our covenant has all the benefits of the Old Testament and more. It's a better covenant!

When people were in covenant in the Old Testament, they reminded one another, "We are in covenant. You have to come and protect me. Your resources are now my resources. All your ability is now my ability." (See Joshua 9; 10:6.)

You may think, "But that was Israel. We are not involved in that covenant." However, according to the Bible, we are! The Bible says we are no longer strangers to the covenant. Paul wrote about Gentiles who once were without Jesus. However, when they accepted Christ, they were no longer aliens or strangers to the promise. Anyone who accepts Christ is part of the covenant.

At that time ye were without Christ, being aliens from the commonwealth of Israel, and

strangers from the covenants of promise, having no hope, and without God in the world: but now in Christ Jesus ye who sometimes were far off are made nigh by the blood of Christ. For he is our peace, who hath made both one, and hath broken down the middle wall of partition between us; having abolished in his flesh the enmity, even the law of commandments contained in ordinances; for to make in himself of twain one new man, so making peace.
(Ephesians 2:12–15)

When you said, "Jesus, come into my life," you became a part of the covenant that God made with His people. You became a part of the covenant that He made with Abraham. You became *"Abraham's seed, and heirs according to the promise"* (Galatians 3:29).

Let me share something else with you. Through Christ, the Abrahamic covenant was fulfilled, ratified, and enacted eternally as a better covenant. The writer to the Hebrews called it a *"new covenant"* (Hebrews 8:8, 13; 12:24), because Christ became our High Priest in the place of a human high priest.

In Hebrews, we find these words:

By so much was Jesus made a surety of a better testament....But this man, because he continueth ever, hath an unchangeable priesthood. (Hebrews 7:22, 24)

Jesus is the surety of our better covenant. He backs it up and has made it good. He guarantees it. He underwrote it as an eternal covenant that is perfect and does not need to be redone.

God Keeps Covenant

When Solomon built the first temple for God, he prayed a dedication prayer.

> *And Solomon stood before the altar of the LORD in the presence of all the congregation of Israel, and spread forth his hands toward heaven: and he said, LORD God of Israel, there is no God like thee, in heaven above, or on earth beneath, who keepest covenant and mercy with thy servants that walk before thee with all their heart.* (1 Kings 8:22–23)

Solomon reminded God of who He is and of what He had promised David about always having a descendant to sit on the throne of Israel, a promise fulfilled in Jesus Christ. Solomon said in 1 Kings 8:25:

> *Therefore now, LORD God of Israel, keep with thy servant David my father that thou promisedst him, saying, There shall not fail thee a man in my sight to sit on the throne of Israel; so that thy children take heed to their way, that they walk before me as thou hast walked before me.*

Notice Solomon said, "You keep covenant; therefore, now, Lord God of Israel, keep Your promise to my father, David." In other words, confirm Your promise. After reminding God of His promise, Solomon called on Him to prove it true by keeping His Word.

When you're backed against the wall, say, "Father, now, verify Your Word. God, I am expecting You to watch over Your Word to perform it. God, I expect You to do exactly what You said You would do."

We are told in Jeremiah 1:12 that God watches over His Word to hasten and perform it. In times of need, you can remind God of His promise mentioned by David in Psalm 37:25: *"I have been young, and now am old; yet have I not seen the righteous forsaken, nor his seed begging bread."*

Approach God Boldly

Psalm 105:8 says that God keeps covenant to a thousand generations. We need to be confident in God's promises and believe that He will do what He said. Faith is confidence in God's Word. If we know His Word and believe He will do it, then we can approach Him boldly to lay hold on those promises. In fact, we are told to do just that. The Bible says for us to come boldly before the throne of grace (Hebrews 4:16).

The writer of Hebrews explained that in order to obtain mercy and find grace to help in time of need, we must come boldly to the Person who can give mercy and grace.

You may be wondering, "How can I build my confidence to approach God boldly?" You approach God knowing that your heart is upright toward Him. Your confidence depends on your faith in God, as well as the condition of your heart. Notice Hezekiah's prayer:

Remember now, O LORD, I beseech thee, how I have walked before thee in truth and with a perfect heart, and have done that which is good in thy sight. (Isaiah 38:3)

I'm not perfect in the natural, but my heart is perfect. My heart desires to please Him, love Him, fulfill His will, and do what He wants me to do. I approach my Father knowing I have a perfect heart toward Him. Therefore, I can come boldly, because I am not coming based on my own works.

Never approach God based on your conduct or actions. I don't care how many good things you do, we are what we are by the grace of God. You approach God based on the blood of Jesus, knowing that you are blood-washed and blood-bought. Isaiah 43:25 says that God blots out our transgressions for His sake, and that He will not remember our sins. If God does not remember them, you shouldn't either.

Don't remind God of your sins and go around beating yourself over the head. Remind Him of His Word, and realize that your sins are blotted out and forgiven, if you have repented. God said that when we confess our sins, He is faithful and just to forgive us and to cleanse us from all unrighteousness (1 John 1:9). That's the power of the covenant. The Devil will try to keep you from coming boldly to the throne by reminding you of your sins and mistakes.

Learn to say, "Devil, get behind me in the name of Jesus. I am blood-washed, and I am blood-bought. I have a blood covenant with the King of Kings and Lord of Lords."

If you keep your heart perfect toward God, know His promises, and remind Him of them, you can expect a miracle.

When you're backed against the wall—

Remind God of His Word.

Chapter 5

Expect a Miracle

When you're backed against the wall, expect miracles. Don't expect things to get worse, and don't expect to go under and lose everything. That's why the first important, imperative point is to take control of your mind. If you do, you're on your way to victory every time. It is impossible for God to lie. If God says He will do something, He will bring it to pass. God is not going to lie.

Evangelist Oral Roberts coined the phrase, "Expect a Miracle." Guess where he got it? He found it in the Word of God. He found that God was a good God, who shows Himself strong when our backs are against the wall. He found that God loves His children far better than any earthly father does (Matthew 7:11).

In 2 Kings 4:1–7, we read about the widow of a prophet's son, who asked Elisha for help, because creditors demanded her two sons be sold into slavery to pay the family's debts. Although she had no income because of losing her husband, she reminded the prophet that her husband was a God-fearing man.

Her husband was dead, her sons were being taken by the creditors, and she had no income. If that's not having your back against the wall, I don't know what is.

Elisha never pitied her. The worst thing in the world that you can do when you're backed against the wall is pity yourself or have someone come along to pity you. Instead, Elisha asked her what she had in her house to sell. She said she had nothing, except a pot of oil. Elisha instructed her to go borrow all the empty containers her neighbors had. He wanted her to borrow all she could find. Then he told her to go into her house and shut the door on her and her sons. Apparently, he didn't believe she needed her neighbors' opinions on what God was about to do. Likewise, the world doesn't need to know everything God is doing for you. The man of God told her to pour oil into all the borrowed vessels from her one pot of oil, and, as she poured, God multiplied the oil. Then the prophet told her to sell the oil, pay her bills, and live on the rest of the money she made. You realize something, don't you? She went to the man of God only because she expected a miracle.

God knows how to multiply within your cabinets. He knows how to stretch your dollars. He knows how to stretch the gas in your automobile. If He needed to, He could make your gas last for two years. At first, you would think your gas gauge was broken because it stayed on full. But He knows your financial situation and when you need a miracle. God knows how to give you a miracle in a way that you will least expect. All things are possible with God (Matthew 19:26). There is nothing too hard for God (Jeremiah 32:17).

Another time the Israelites found their backs against the wall was when there was famine in Samaria, causing inflation, which led to widespread famine in the land. Starving people became so desperate that they began eating babies.

Out of frustration, the king of Israel threatened to behead Elisha and sent word by a messenger to the prophet's house. Elisha sent word back to the king that God would turn Samaria's famine into prosperity within 24 hours.

God caused the Syrian army to hear the sound of a multitude of chariots and horses as four leprous men approached their camp. Fearing they were being ambushed by their enemies, the Syrian soldiers fled, leaving all their food, clothing, and other valuables behind. When the lepers sent word to the king about what had happened, the Israelites went to the Syrians' camp and took everything. (See 2 Kings 6:24–7:20.)

Throughout the Bible, we read how God's people faced dilemmas and devastations. But whenever their backs were against the wall and their hearts were perfect toward God, He powerfully demonstrated His Word on their behalf.

I don't care if your electricity is about to get cut off or your car insurance is on the verge of being canceled, God knows how to pay your bills. However, to receive your miracle, you must cooperate with God and willingly work extra hours, if God makes them available. If God provides overtime for you, work the overtime. He knows what He's doing.

Don't view the opportunity for extra work as the boss leaning on you or the Devil trying to keep you from getting off work. Often, that's God's way of bringing you out of a financial dilemma, and laziness or a wrong attitude can cause you to miss it.

Ephesians 3:20 says that God does exceeding abundantly above all that we ask or think. God doesn't *barely* put you over. He puts you over *abundantly.* God knows how to make His children look good. Jesus came so that we might have life and have it more abundantly (John 10:10). Remember the widow had enough oil to sell that would get her out of debt and that would provide enough for her to live on for the rest of her life!

When you're backed against the wall—

Expect a miracle.

Chapter 6

Go to Sleep

When you're backed against the wall and you have done all you can do, go to sleep. This demonstrates confidence in God. God doesn't expect His people to pace the floor at night or pull their hair out because they are frantically worrying. He expects us to go to sleep just like usual. Isn't that the way it is when you take someone at his word? Well, God cannot lie. It is vain for us not to sleep. Let's look at Psalm 127:1–2:

> *Except the LORD build the house, they labour in vain that build it: except the LORD keep the city, the watchman waketh but in vain. It is vain for you to rise up early, to sit up late, to eat the bread of sorrows: for so he giveth his beloved sleep.*

Let's look at a scriptural account of going to sleep when you're backed against the wall. In Acts 12 King Herod had James, the brother of John, killed. Then, because he saw it pleased the Jews, he arrested the apostle Peter and intended to kill him after the Passover celebration that year. Acts 12:5–6 says,

Peter therefore was kept in prison: but prayer was made without ceasing of the church unto God for him. And when Herod would have brought him forth, the same night Peter was sleeping.

The night before he was to be executed, Peter was sleeping! How many Christians today would sleep the night before their heads were to be chopped off? Those who knew and believed the Word would. Peter remembered the promise Jesus made to him that implied he would live to be an old man. (See John 21:18.)

Peter thought to himself, "I am still young. I am going to sleep. Herod can't kill me, because it is impossible for Jesus to lie." Peter had lived and traveled with Jesus for three-and-a-half years, and he knew that Jesus was a man of His word. When Jesus spoke, circumstances changed. When Jesus commanded blind eyes to open, they opened. When He cursed the fig tree, it dried up. When He told Lazarus to come out of the grave, he came. When He prophesied that Peter would deny Him, it happened.

So when He told Peter he would live to be an old man, Peter knew he couldn't die a young man, not if he believed Jesus. So he went to sleep, chained and lying between two soldiers. But, praise God, the same night, an angel of God was sent and set Peter free.

My friend, listen to me. When you take God's Word and put it in your heart and act like God cannot lie, angels, the Holy Spirit, the Lord Jesus, and God Himself will spring you free. You'll come out of your prison, off that wall, set free by the power of God. God's Word and integrity make us able to sleep soundly every night. Let me remind you of one of His promises that should make you sleep well tonight.

> *But now thus saith the LORD that created thee, O Jacob, and he that formed thee, O Israel. Fear not: for I have redeemed thee, I have called thee by thy name; thou art mine. When thou passest through the waters, I will be with thee; and through the rivers, they shall not overflow thee: when thou walkest through the fire, thou shalt not be burned; neither shall the flame kindle upon thee. For I am the LORD thy God, the Holy One of Israel, thy Saviour: I gave Egypt for thy ransom, Ethiopia and Seba for thee.* (Isaiah 43:1–3)

> *Since thou wast precious in my sight, thou hast been honourable, and I have loved thee: therefore will I give men for thee, and people for thy life.* (Isaiah 43:4)

God will go out of His way to protect you—even if it means wiping out an unbeliever who has come against you. Once you take Him at His Word, the oppressor will be able to fight against you for only so long.

Many people do not understand God in that sense. They don't understand that if God has to bring divine judgment on a man for your sake, He will. If He has to remove presidents, supervisors, or coworkers just for you, He will. God loves you, and you're called by His name.

The Bible says that our God is a consuming fire (Hebrews 12:29), and *"it is a fearful thing to fall into the hands of the living God"* (Hebrews 10:31).

It's time for you to receive what God has made available to you. It's not time to let the Devil rob you. Get into the Word of God, learn His promises to you, and receive them by faith. When you do that, be like Peter, and regardless of what it looks like, go to sleep. Your miracle is coming.

When you're backed against the wall—

Go to sleep.

Chapter 7

Don't Count Your Life Dear to Yourself

When you're backed against the wall, make sure you don't count your life dear to yourself. If you place too much value on your own life, you will make wrong decisions.

> *And they overcame him by the blood of the Lamb, and by the word of their testimony; and they loved not their lives unto the death.*
> (Revelation 12:11)

This Scripture refers to end-time martyrs who valued the ministry above their own lives. While few of us will face the degree of suffering they had to endure, the same principle applies. In order to defeat the Enemy, Christians must make satisfying their flesh such a low priority that they never compromise their righteousness.

Allowing your flesh to rule you will cause you to seek what appears to be the quickest, easiest, and most painless way out of hardships. If you count your life dear to yourself, you will back away from the will of God when situations become difficult. When hard times come, you will begin to look for alternatives that make it comfortable for you. That might even mean lying, or worse.

When I was a child, I recall grown-ups telling their children to lie to creditors, saying they weren't at home or that they were asleep. In order to win when you're backed against the wall, you must be determined to face adversity. If necessary, go to your creditors, explain your situation, and work out a payment plan with them. Your attitude must be, "If you must take my car, then take it; but one day, I'll pay the money I owe you. If I lose my house, then I lose it. I will not connive, scheme, or lie to save it, because I can get another house. I won't count my life so extremely important to myself."

To receive a miracle when you're backed against the wall, you must place God's Word and walking Christlike above your desires, feelings, and thoughts.

The apostle Paul often found his back against the wall. In one instance recorded in Acts 20, he spoke about the trials he faced.

> *And now, behold, I go bound in the spirit unto Jerusalem, not knowing the things that shall befall me there: save that the Holy Ghost witnesseth in every city, saying that bonds and affliction abide me.*
>
> (Acts 20:22–23)

In the next verse, we see Paul's attitude toward those trials.

> *Neither count I my life dear unto myself, so that I might finish my course with joy, and the*

*ministry, which I have received of the Lord
Jesus, to testify the gospel of the grace of
God.* (Acts 20:24)

Despite having to endure one trial after another, he was determined not to quit, give up, or
grow weary in his mind. Paul's life wasn't easy,
yet he stayed focused on God's promises and
kept his joy. You'll be able to do the same if you:

• Know that your Redeemer lives (Job 19:25).
• Know that His grace is sufficient for you in all
  situations (2 Corinthians 12:9).
• Are fully persuaded that what He has prom-
  ised, He is able also to perform (Romans 4:21).
• Know who you are and what your rights and
  authority are in Christ (Mark 16:16–18).
• Know that you are divinely protected (Psalm
  91).
• Know the power of the blood of Jesus (1 John
  1:7).
• Know the power of His name (Acts 4:12).

I know a lot of Christians today who, unlike
Paul, couldn't say, *"But none of these things move
me"* (Acts 20:24). That's because every difficult
situation moves them. They're moved to the telephone to call everybody they know to pray. They
begin confessing all kinds of negative thoughts or
just cry and give up. But Paul said that nothing
moved him off his determined course in Christ.

The Bible tells us to think highly of ourselves,
but not more highly than we ought (Romans 12:3).
However, many Christians think more highly of

themselves, and it causes them to count their lives dear to themselves, often leading to major mistakes. They regard their lives and lifestyles too highly.

They refuse to wait for the blessings of God. They want two cars, a house full of furniture, several televisions, and several telephones *now*. They can't defer gratification of the flesh. They have to have it all *now*.

When my wife and I first got married, we ate on a little card table and sat on a travel trunk because we didn't have chairs. Most people would have gone in debt to buy a dinette set, but not us. We were determined to wait on God, not let pride run our lives.

We didn't have to live that way too long, because we didn't count our lives dear to ourselves. Because we were willing to do without in order to get ahead, God began blessing us.

A lot of people don't give to God or release assets to God because they count their lives too dear to themselves.

The rich young ruler who came to Jesus asking what he had to do to be saved decided he couldn't sell his possessions and give to the poor as Jesus had instructed him. (See Luke 18:18–25.) He was too concerned about his own survival. Yet, if he had followed Jesus' directive, he would have survived and been blessed like never before, according to the following Scripture.

And Jesus answered and said, Verily I say unto you, There is no man that hath left house, or brethren, or sisters, or father, or

> *mother, or wife, or children, or lands, for my*
> *sake, and the gospel's, but he shall receive*
> *an hundredfold now in this time, houses, and*
> *brethren, and sisters, and mothers, and chil-*
> *dren, and lands, with persecutions; and in the*
> *world to come eternal life.* (Mark 10:29–30)

Some Christians don't tithe because of fear of going without, living a lower quality of life, or, simply put, being in love with themselves. Yet God says,

> *Bring ye all the tithes into the storehouse, that*
> *there may be meat in mine house, and prove*
> *me now herewith, saith the LORD of hosts, if I*
> *will not open you the windows of heaven, and*
> *pour you out a blessing, that there shall not*
> *be room enough to receive it. And I will re-*
> *buke the devourer for your sakes, and he*
> *shall not destroy the fruits of your ground;*
> *neither shall your vine cast her fruit before*
> *the time in the field, saith the LORD of hosts.*
> (Malachi 3:10–11)

Blessed is the person who trusts in God. Blessed is the one who will defer self-gratification to do the will of God now. Blessed is the man who says, "I give my tithes to You, God, regardless of what I lose and what I can't buy."

How often do unbelievers say, "What's a car? I'll get another one." Yet some believers react to the loss of a car just like they would react to the loss of a loved one.

If you can't buy new clothes for a year, just keep wearing the same old duds and remind God of His Word concerning meeting your needs and giving you the desires of your heart. After you have reminded Him of His Word, wait for the vine to *"cast* [its] *fruit"* (Malachi 3:11) at the right season. Don't force the season. Wait on it!

Let's consider two other examples from the Bible. An Old Testament prophet named Balaam got in trouble with God by counting his life dear to himself. God told him specifically not to go to the king of Moab to curse the children of Israel. But after the Moabites offered him more money and riches, he said, *"Stay here tonight, that I may know what more the LORD will say to me"* (Numbers 22:19 NKJV).

In the end, Balaam went to the king of Moab, but he didn't curse Israel, because God wouldn't let him. Instead, he pronounced a blessing on them. However, he warned the Israelites that they could be tempted to sin and could be destroyed by Moabite women. A number of the Israelite men committed fornication with the daughters of Moab and were lured into worshipping and making sacrifices to idols. As a result, judgment came on Israel in the form of a plague that killed 24,000 people. (See Numbers 25:1–9.)

Balaam died by the sword when the Israelites later fought against the Midianites just before Moses died (Numbers 31:8). In the book of Revelation, people who ministered or prophesied for money and encouraged God's people to participate in the world's pleasures are described as *"them that hold the doctrine of Balaam"* (Revelation 2:14). Holding their lives dear to themselves cost them dearly!

Gehazi, Elisha's servant, is another prime example of what happens when people put their wants and desires ahead of God. In 2 Kings 5, Naaman, the captain of the host of the king of Syria, came to Samaria to see the prophet Elisha. A servant girl, taken from Israel in slavery, had told him that Elisha could heal him of leprosy.

After Naaman received his healing through Elisha's ministry, he was so grateful. He tried to give Elisha gifts, but Elisha refused to accept them.

Gehazi thought his master was crazy for not accepting Naaman's gifts. He probably thought to himself: "I can't believe the man of God is refusing to accept these valuable gifts. Naaman has offered him a small fortune in money and expensive clothes.

"Since he doesn't want it, I'll take it," Gehazi thought, and he began to plot how to get it. As soon as Elisha turned his back and Naaman had traveled up the road out of sight, Gehazi went after Naaman and lied, saying that Elisha had changed his mind and now wanted the money and clothing.

Immediately, Elisha knew what his servant had done and asked him where he had been. Again, Gehazi had to lie to cover his tracks. His first mistake was counting his life and his desires too dear to himself. Even then, if he had confessed and repented, he might have been spared. Instead, he was rebuked by Elisha and cursed with leprosy. Read what Elisha said to Gehazi:

Went not mine heart with thee, when the man turned again from his chariot to meet thee? Is

45

it a time to receive money, and to receive garments, and oliveyards, and vineyards, and sheep, and oxen, and menservants, and maidservants? The leprosy therefore of Naaman shall cleave unto thee, and unto thy seed for ever. And he went out from his presence a leper as white as snow.

(2 Kings 5:26–27)

That bag of silver and two changes of expensive clothes cost Gehazi his health and the health of his descendants. When God said, *"Unto thy seed for ever,"* He meant forever!

How many people have lied because they counted their lives too dear to themselves? Death is still *"the wages of sin,"* and *"the gift of God is* [still] *eternal life through Jesus Christ our Lord"* (Romans 6:23).

Satan is a liar and the Father of Lies (John 8:44). Whenever you are tempted to lie because of situations, realize that the Devil is oppressing or tempting you. You must cast down imaginations and say out loud, "In the name of Jesus, let me go, Satan. I am going the way of the Word."

Loving the World Hinders Your Love of God

If you love the world and things in the world, the love of the Father is not in you (1 John 2:15).

Temporal things are subject to change, and the Bible tells us not to look at the things that are seen, but at things that are not seen, *"for the things which are seen are temporal; but the things which are not seen are eternal"* (2 Corinthians 4:18).

Many people who are seriously in debt spend lots of money on pleasure. They go out to eat, buy snacks and sodas (unnecessary food), bowl in leagues, pay costly golf fees, and go on shopping sprees as if they owe no one anything. You must put first things first. Defer gratifying your desires for six months or a year to get your debts paid. Deny your flesh for as long as is needed, and you'll come out mature, stronger in the things of God, and confident that the Word works.

Sometimes pride is the cause of our loving ourselves too much. We don't want to be embarrassed and wouldn't want anyone to know that our electricity got turned off. That's understandable, but we shouldn't do things that are wrong that will put us deeper in a hole just to keep the lights on.

Jesus said that the kingdom of God operates like a man who plants seed. (See Matthew 13:18–23.) The man goes to bed and gets up, goes to bed and gets up, and finally, there is a blade. Then there is an ear, and then there is the full corn in the ear. In between the blade and the ear, you might have to endure some things, but the full ear is coming.

Endure Hardness

The word *endure* means you are going to fight through your situation. You are going to do what you have to do. You can't just cop out and look for ways around it.

Thou therefore, my son, be strong in the grace that is in Christ Jesus. And the things

47

that thou hast heard of me among many wit-nesses, the same commit thou to faithful men, who shall be able to teach others. Thou therefore endure hardness, as a good soldier of Jesus Christ. No man that warreth entan-gleth himself with the affairs of this life; that he may please him who hath chosen him to be a soldier. (2 Timothy 2:1–4)

"Hardness," referred to in the passage above, actually means hardships. Nobody wants to ride in those kinds of ships. But Paul told Timothy to endure hardship as a good soldier of Jesus Christ. Jesus said that in the world we would have tribu-lation (John 16:33). We don't seek tribulation, but it comes; and when it comes, we endure.

How willing are you to do what it takes to come out of your bad circumstances? Are you determined to endure and to make your way through whatever comes? Are you willing to do without certain luxuries, if the situation calls for it? Are you willing to resist blessing yourself and waiting for the blessings of God? We must be willing to do whatever it takes to get our backs off the wall.

When you're backed against the wall—

Don't count your life dear to yourself.

Chapter 8

Evaluate the Spirit in Which You Walk

When you're backed against the wall, all kinds of spirits will try to attack, control, manipulate, and dominate you. You must decide not to allow ungodly spirits to gain control of you. In order to evaluate the Spirit in which you walk, you must first determine if you're being guided by the Holy Spirit or some other spirit. First John 4:1–2 says,

> Beloved, believe not every spirit, but try the spirits whether they are of God: because many false prophets are gone out into the world. Hereby know ye the Spirit of God: Every spirit that confesseth that Jesus Christ is come in the flesh is of God.   (1 John 4:1–2)

During trials and tribulations, ungodly spirits try to build strongholds in believers' minds. If you begin reacting to trouble in an ungodly manner, then you have opened yourself up to ungodly spirits. These spirits appear in different forms, including:

- A spirit of fear—We know a spirit of fear is not from God, because the Bible specifically says God has *"not given us the spirit of fear; but of power, and of love, and of a sound mind"* (2 Timothy 1:7).

- A spirit of infirmity—This causes some people to react to hardships by getting sick.

- A lying spirit—This causes people to exaggerate and fabricate, just as Gehazi did.

- A spirit of compromise—This will cause you to waiver and become double minded in order to make provisions for your flesh. James 1:7–8 says that a double-minded man will not receive anything from the Lord.

- A spirit of disobedience—This will lead you to ignore God's Word and His instructions to you so that you can handle situations your own way. Paul wrote to the church at Ephesus concerning the spirit of disobedience:

> *And you hath he quickened, who were dead in trespasses and sins: wherein in time past ye walked according to the course of this world, according to the prince of the power of the air, the spirit that now worketh in the children of disobedience.* (Ephesians 2:1–2)

When one of my children was struggling with obedience, I wouldn't let a day pass without having that child make confessions of faith specifically on obedience. The confessions were along these lines:

"I am free from a spirit of disobedience. I obey my parents in the Lord. I am a child of obedience. I am not stubborn. I am not strong-willed against my parents' teachings."

A spirit of disobedience really does exist. When you're backed against the wall and you're all shaken up, that spirit can seize control of you if you aren't careful and alert. For example, instead of tithing, you'll use that money for something else.

Decide

When you're backed against the wall, you must decide which way you'll go, what kind of spirit will operate in your life, and what you will allow to control and dominate you.

We must decide to walk in the spirit of faith all the time, especially when our backs are against the wall. God won't push a button to make you walk in faith. That's your choice. Everyone who is born again has the spirit of faith. As Paul wrote,

We having the same spirit of faith, according as it is written, I believed, and therefore have I spoken; we also believe, and therefore speak. (2 Corinthians 4:13)

When my back is against the wall, I choose the spirit of faith. I don't choose fear, disobedience, lying, compromise, or deceit; nor do I choose to lie down. In 1 John 5:4, John explained that we should walk in the spirit of faith: *"This is the victory that overcometh the world, even our faith."* Know that your faith will overcome any trial or situation. Overcoming faith belongs to us if we belong to God.

You need to understand something before I go any further, and that is: When you're backed against the wall, a major tactic of the Devil is to convince you that your problem is unique and that your faith is not strong enough to overcome it.

If you don't guard your thoughts, you'll begin to believe no one has ever faced anything like this, and you're the only one in the whole world going through anything of this magnitude. But that's a lie. Satan is the Father of Lies, and the truth is not in him. Your situation is not unique. Ecclesiastes 1:9 says there is nothing new under the sun.

Do you have a lust problem? That's nothing new. Are you unemployed? Nothing new. Are you dealing with rebellious children? Nothing new. Do you have financial problems? Nothing new. But the Devil will try to convince you that you're the only one with past-due bills.

He's a liar! You simply have to make up your mind about who you are in Christ. Begin to tell yourself and the Devil, "I am a winner! I win, hallelujah! I choose ahead of time to win. I know I am going to win now. Thanks be to God, who always causes me to triumph in Christ Jesus!"

The Spirit of God said through Paul, *"There hath no temptation taken you but such as is common to man"* (1 Corinthians 10:13). *"Common"* means familiar. In other words, this is the norm. Whatever you are facing, it's not unique. So don't lie down thinking you're alone or that nobody understands. Probably a million or more people right now could understand.

We see in 1 Kings 19:9–18 where God had to straighten Elijah out for thinking his situation was unique. He was whining to God and having a real pity party. He complained that he was the only one left serving God. God responded, *"There are seven thousand more"* (v. 18). I can hear God saying, "Now, hush your mouth, boy."

The Spirit of Faith

You're probably wondering how you can tell if you are walking in the spirit of faith. Well, it's not hard. There are two indicators: what you say and what you do.

People who walk in the spirit of faith speak to themselves and their mountains, and they "do" the Word. They talk, and they do. I am reminded of David, whose back was against the wall many times in life-or-death situations. At one time, even his own men wanted to kill him. They were furious because while he and his men were away in battle, enemy troops raided their camp, taking their wives and children captive. (See 1 Samuel 30:1–25.)

Their town was burned, and all their goods were taken. After returning home and finding their wives and possessions gone, David's men, who had been fighting with him now, threatened to kill him. David must have been drained emotionally, because his family had also been taken, and his men were blaming him for all this misfortune. He must have felt discouraged, disheartened, and defeated, but the Bible says David encouraged himself (talk), and he pursued his enemies and recovered all (do).

According to Hebrews 11, we have the same spirit of faith that was in those Old Testament heroes and heroines. Many others besides David walked in the spirit of faith. People who have the spirit of faith talk to themselves and they take action when their backs are against the wall. They encourage themselves by making faith confessions, such as:

- I am a world overcomer through Jesus (John 16:33).
- I can do all things through Christ who strengthens me (Philippians 4:13).
- I am coming out of this situation, because I have the mind of Christ (1 Corinthians 2:16).
- I am the head and not the tail (Deuteronomy 28:13).
- Greater is He who is in me, than he who is in the world (1 John 4:4).
- God will never leave me or forsake me (Hebrews 13:5).
- I am a giver, and my God will supply all my needs according to His riches in glory by Christ Jesus (Philippians 4:19).
- I am strong in the Lord and in the power of His might (Ephesians 6:10).

David spoke to himself in Psalm 42:11, asking his soul, *"Why art thou disquieted within me?"* His soul probably answered, "Well, they have taken your wife, they have taken your children, they have taken your men's wives and goods, and they have burned the city." Answering himself, David said, *"Hope thou in God"* (v. 11). Did you know that one of the ways you lose is by not talking to yourself?

He told his soul to bless the Lord in other verses in Psalms. The Spirit of faith will cause you to stand still and bless the Lord when your emotions tell you to do differently.

In Psalm 103:2, David told us not to forget God's benefits. Thinking about God's benefits will stir you up quickly and get you back on the right track. You won't know if you are walking in the spirit of faith unless you listen to yourself. Ask yourself:

- What do I say when the chips are down and other believers aren't around?
- What do I murmur under my breath to supervisors and those who've offended me?
- What do I utter in frustration while driving?
- What would I say if I were about to lose my husband, wife, job, or valuable possessions?

Your responses in crises reflect the spirit in which you are operating. When you're not walking in the spirit of faith, you will most likely walk in the spirit of compromise, the spirit of fear, the spirit of disobedience, and the spirit of lying.

Let's stay away from all spirits that are not of God. To walk in the spirit of faith, you must tell yourself what God says about your situation. Talk to your problem, and do the Word.

When you're backed against the wall—

Walk in a spirit of faith.

Chapter 9

Remember Who the Devil Is, Who You Are, and Who God Is

In some church circles, believers are told to concentrate on who God is and who they are in Christ without ever being told to know their spiritual Enemy, the Devil. Yet, in preparing for battle, successful soldiers spend some time learning about their enemy. As a member of God's army, not only do you need to know who God is and who you are in Christ, but you must also be able to know and recognize the traits and tactics of the Devil. We must not be ignorant of Satan or his devices (2 Corinthians 2:11).

Unfortunately, some believers have been deceived by the images Hollywood has portrayed of the Devil to the point of not being able to recognize his true attributes. The Bible describes him as a thief, liar, deceiver, murderer, accuser, destroyer, defeated foe, and a fallen angel, who has no power over believers. When you come to grips with who he is, you will no longer allow him to intimidate you or rob you of your blessings.

Just Who Is the Devil?

Remember! The Devil is a liar and the Father of Lies. Jesus said these words to the scribes and Pharisees in John 8:44:

Ye are of your father the devil, and the lusts of your father ye will do. He was a murderer from the beginning, and abode not in the truth, because there is no truth in him. When he speaketh a lie, he speaketh of his own: for he is a liar, and the father of it.

When the Devil says you are going under, remember that he is a liar, and there is no truth in him. When he tells you that you are going to lose everything, don't believe his lie.

First Peter 5:8 tells us that Satan walks around like a roaring lion, *"seeking whom he may devour."* He can't just huff, puff, and blow your house down anytime he wants. He has to seek someone whom he can devour. He does not have the authority or the ability to do whatever he wants, whenever he wants, but he wants to deceive you into thinking he does. That way he can get you focusing on your situation and circumstances. He tries to convince you that your hardships will last forever and that you'll never amount to anything in life. He'll tell you that you will never come out of debt or get healed. But remember: he's a liar! There is no truth in him.

The Word of God tells us that *"the things which are seen are temporal"* (2 Corinthians 4:18), and *"they that observe lying vanities forsake their own mercy"* (Jonah 2:8). Everything is subject to change, and because of this, you must not focus on what you see or what you're going through. You must guard your mind when trouble comes. Otherwise, you will forget that the Devil is a liar, and that your obstacles and hurdles are temporary.

When the Devil approaches you with lies, guard your mind by reminding yourself: "I've already made it. I belong to Jesus! I am on the winning team. I will *'not die, but live, and declare the works of the LORD'* (Psalm 118:17)." Then, remind the Devil that he is a liar. Remind him that he lied to you last week, last night, and this morning. Remind him that he has been lying to you all your life. The last thing he wants you to remember when you're backed against the wall is that you are already on the winning team and that he is a liar!

Don't Surrender to a Defeated Foe

Colossians 2:15 reveals the Devil as a defeated foe. Jesus handed Satan his defeat when He died on the cross and rose from the dead with all power in His hand. Yet despite his defeat, Satan has caused a lot of destruction in the earth.

The Father of Lies has seduced people into carrying out much of his plan simply because they take him at his word and believe his lies. Those who are deceived into believing Satan are tricked into carrying out his desires. Much of the destruction he instigates would never occur if he were not able to convince anyone by deception to do his wicked works for him.

Satan is not equal to God in power or anything else. As a created being, he is not all-powerful or all-knowing or omnipresent. He is not a god, although he would like to be; he constantly attempts to get mankind to treat him as one.

The New Testament makes it very clear that Satan was defeated once and for all by Jesus Christ. Furthermore, Jesus revealed to John in the book of Revelation that Satan, the deceiver, will be *"cast into the lake of fire and brimstone, where the beast and the false prophet are, and shall be tormented day and night for ever and ever"* (Revelation 20:10).

The Devil is doomed. Not only is he doomed, but also all the fallen angels that sinned with him are doomed, for

> *God spared not the angels that sinned, but cast them down to hell, and delivered them into chains of darkness, to be reserved unto judgment.* (2 Peter 2:4)

Jesus told the Devil it was over, and it was over! He demonstrated to His heavenly Father, the angelic host, and the Holy Spirit that Satan was whipped forever, and then He went on to make a show of him openly in the realm of the spirit (Colossians 2:15). I want you to know that Satan still remembers his defeat. He still remembers the Lordship of Jesus and who Jesus is.

I am certain that every time Satan hears the name of Jesus, he remembers! Every time a believer says "the blood of Jesus," he remembers. Although Satan is the author of every tragedy, devastation, and seemingly insurmountable situation, you must remember that he is already conquered. Jesus is Lord over your situation!

Defeated and Destroyed

Satan has not only been beaten and defeated, but also destroyed:

> *Forasmuch then as the children are partakers of flesh and blood, he also himself likewise took part of the same; that through death he might destroy him that had the power of death, that is, the devil.* (Hebrews 2:14)

This doesn't mean that Satan doesn't exist, but rather that he has been brought to a place of nothingness. Jesus took on the human characteristics of flesh and blood in order to gain legal access to the earthly realm. It was only through His death that He could destroy the Devil and his works. If you forget who the Devil is, he will have an effect on your life that he has no business having. Those who do remember can know and say with confidence, *"No weapon that is formed against* [me] *shall prosper"* (Isaiah 54:17).

Jesus said in Luke 10:18, *"I beheld Satan as lightning fall from heaven."* Well, I think I'll remember that! I'll say to the Devil, "Satan, you aren't what you used to be. You lost your place when you fell from heaven. You have no authority over me anymore." Some Christians will say, "You'd better not talk to the Devil like that. Watch out because he'll get you." Watch out for what?

The Bible says the works of the Devil have been destroyed: *"For this purpose was the Son of God manifested, that he might destroy the works of the devil"* (1 John 3:8).

When the Devil comes against me, trying to back me against the wall, I remember that he is defeated. He can't shut my mouth, and he can't shut yours, either. The more you say it, the more he backs off, and the more you produce victory in the realm of the spirit. Remember: the Devil is a defeated foe, and Jesus is Lord!

You Are an Ambassador

The second part of this equation is remembering who you are in Christ. Who are you? Second Corinthians 5:20 describes us as *"ambassadors for Christ."* An ambassador holds a position of authority. We represent the King of Kings and the Lord of Lords. That means we have authority and power. In the next verse we are described as being *"the righteousness of God in* [Christ Jesus]*"* (v. 21).

As ambassadors of Christ, we represent who He is and what He has. Jesus has *"all power...in heaven and in earth"* (Matthew 28:18). If my back is against the wall, I must remember that I represent the King of Kings, the One who defeated the Devil and has *"all power...in heaven and in earth."*

I must remember that I am God's righteousness in Christ Jesus and no longer a sinner. I have been saved by grace. In Mark 16:15–18, Jesus commissioned us to go in His name. We are not to go and lose to the Devil.

A World Overcomer

Not only are we ambassadors of Christ and God's righteousness in Christ Jesus, but we are also overcomers in this world:

Ye are of God, little children, and have over-come them: because greater is he that is in you, than he that is in the world. (1 John 4:4)

We are overcomers against every spirit that denies the fact that Jesus came in the flesh. The Bible states that every spirit that does not confess *"that Jesus Christ is come in the flesh is not of God: and this is that spirit of antichrist"* (v. 3). We are overcomers against every evil and wicked spirit that fights against us. We need to remember that!

You are of God and therefore a child of God's: *"Behold, what manner of love the Father hath bestowed upon us, that we should be called the sons of God"* (1 John 3:1). You are a citizen of heaven, redeemed from the curse of the law and translated into the kingdom of God's dear Son.

You may need to remind yourself of this by saying it one hundred times, but get it down in your spirit. Say this out loud right now: "I'm of God and not of this world. God calls me His child. I am not a beggar or a worm. I am not poor or weak. I am not stupid or dumb. I'm not incompetent. I am of God, and I am His child."

More than a Conqueror

In Romans 8:37, Paul reminded the Christians at Rome that they were *"more than conquerors through him that loved* [them]." The same is true of us today. In verse 35, Paul mentioned the kind of hardships that might put your back against the wall: *"tribulation, or distress, or persecution, or famine, or nakedness, or peril, or sword* [war and violence]."

Every one of those things that Paul mentioned is temporary, and in every one of those situations, we are already conquerors. We must remember who we are and that we have more than enough of God's anointing inside us to handle any situation. It is resident within us.

John wrote in Revelation 1:6 that God has made us *"kings and priests."* We have been raised *"up together, and made* [to] *sit together in heavenly places in Christ Jesus"* (Ephesians 2:6). With all of this, how can we not win!

You are more than a conqueror (Romans 8:37). You are the head and not the tail, and you are above and not beneath (Deuteronomy 28:13). You are blessed going out and blessed coming in (Psalm 121:8). You are blessed in the city and blessed in the field (Deuteronomy 28:3). You are a king and a priest unto God (Revelation 1:6). You are of God.

When you're backed against the wall, begin to say out loud: "I am sitting in heavenly places in Christ Jesus. I am far above principalities, power, might, dominion, and every name that is named, not only in this world, but in the world to come. (See Ephesians 1:20–21.) I am a child of God, adopted and made a *'new creature'* (2 Corinthians 5:17) through the eternal blood covenant. I will not fear a created being who never was a child of

God or was not made in the image of God. He not only is in rebellion against God, but also is the instigator of everything that is against God."

These thoughts inspire and motivate me. They turn the picture around for me, and I believe they will do the same for you.

The Almighty God

In any given situation, you must remember who God is, especially if the Devil is trying to put your back against the wall. When Abraham was 99 years old, the Lord appeared to him and said, *"I am the Almighty God"* (Genesis 17:1). In other words, God was saying, "I'm not just mighty, but I have *all* might in My hands."

That is what we need to remember if our backs are against the wall. When the Devil says, "How are you going to get out of this one?" you say, "By almighty God! By the One who is all-powerful and has all might in His hands."

King Nebuchadnezzar asked Shadrach, Meshach, and Abednego how they were going to escape the fiery furnace, and what god would deliver them out of his hands. They simply replied, *"Our God whom we serve is able to deliver us from the burning fiery furnace, and he will deliver us out of thine hand, O king"* (Daniel 3:17).

Those young Hebrews said, "We don't even have to think about this. We are not going to bow; nor will we burn. We have a God who is mightier than the furnace you are going to put us in, even though it is seven times hotter than usual." (See verse 19.)

The fire in the furnace was so hot that it killed the king's men who put the Hebrew boys into it. (See verse 22.) And when it seemed like the same would happen to Shadrach, Meshach, and Abednego, the Bible says King Nebuchadnezzar said these words to his counselors,

> *Did not we cast three men bound into the midst of the fire? They answered and said unto the king, True, O king. He answered and said, Lo, I see four men loose, walking in the midst of the fire, and they have no hurt; and the form of the fourth is like the Son of God.*
> (Daniel 3:24–25)

King Nebuchadnezzar saw that not a hair on Shadrach's, Meshach's, or Abednego's head was burned and that their clothes didn't even smell of smoke. He realized the fire had no power over their bodies and proclaimed them *"servants of the most high God"* (v. 26).

The Only God

Look at what God says about Himself in Isaiah 45:5–6, 12:

> *I am the LORD, and there is none else, there is no God beside me: I girded thee, though thou hast not known me: that they may know from the rising of the sun, and from the west, that there is none beside me. I am the LORD, and there is none else....I have made the earth, and created man upon it: I, even my*

hands, have stretched out the heavens, and all their host have I commanded.

It's good to remember that you serve the only God. Throughout Isaiah 45, God said, *"I am the LORD,"* or *"I am God, and there is none else."* It's a good chapter to meditate on to develop your faith in who God is.

The God of Our Salvation

Isaiah 12:2 says, *"Behold, God is my salvation; I will trust, and not be afraid: for the LORD JEHOVAH is my strength and my song; he also is become my salvation."*

Only God can save you when you're backed against the wall. David expressed this reality in the midst of his trouble: *"The LORD is my light and my salvation; whom shall I fear? The LORD is the strength of my life, of whom shall I be afraid?"* (Psalm 27:1).

As I remember these verses I say, "Father, I thank You because You are my God. You are my salvation. You are my strength, and You are my song. I will trust You and will not be afraid. You are my light. I will not walk in darkness. I will not stumble and fall because You are my light, and You are my salvation. No matter how bad it looks, Lord, I am going to be delivered. My situation that seems like a fiery furnace is only temporary. No matter how dismal it looks or how many of my foes are closing in on me, You will save me. When my enemies come upon me to destroy me, they will stumble and fall because You are my light and my salvation."

In Exodus 15:1–3, Moses and the children of Israel rejoiced in the fact that God was their salvation:

> Then sang Moses and the children of Israel this song unto the LORD, and spake, saying, I will sing unto the LORD, for he hath triumphed gloriously: the horse and his rider hath he thrown into the sea. The LORD is my strength and song, and he is become my salvation: he is my God, and I will prepare him an habitation; my father's God, and I will exalt him. The LORD is a man of war: the LORD is his name.

When the Devil has you backed against a wall, come off that wall shouting, "I am coming against you in the name of the Lord who is a Man of war." The Devil will back off quickly, and I mean quickly! The Devil has had too many confrontations with Jesus, the almighty God. He also knows that he has lost every one of them.

Every time you say, "I am coming against you in the name of the Lord, the Man of war," you scare the Devil. He will run from you in terror. You need to understand the kind of God you serve. When you do, you can start a fight with the Devil, knowing you are prepared to do battle in the name of the Lord.

Our Hope and Our Peace

In Exodus 15:26, God said, *"I am the LORD that healeth thee."* That verse is especially important to remember when the doctor says your condition is terminal and gives you six months to live, or if he diagnoses you with a degenerative disease that will cause your life to slowly ebb away. God's promises produce hope and peace.

The apostle Paul was en route to Rome to be tried when a severe storm arose, threatening the lives of everyone on board ship. (See Acts 27:6–44.) However, Paul said that an angel appeared to him from God, saying, *"Fear not, Paul; thou must be brought before Caesar: and, lo, God hath given thee all them that sail with thee"* (v. 24).

Because of Paul, everyone on board was saved, although the ship and all of its cargo were lost. When you're backed against the wall, you have to know that you belong to God.

In Romans 15:13, Paul called Him *"the God of hope."* If you belong to God, there's always hope. Regardless of the circumstances—whether it's a terminal illness or being shipwrecked at sea—God always endeavors to stir up hope inside you because He is *"the God of hope."*

Romans 15:33 refers to God as *"the God of peace."* Our God of peace *"shall bruise Satan under your feet shortly"* (Romans 16:20). In the natural, Satan will literally be under your feet as you look to God to give you your victory.

God Is Our Source

Finally, when you're backed against the wall, remember that God is your Source. He is El Shaddai, the almighty One; and Jehovah Jireh, your Provider. Do not look to your husband, your wife, your employer, your grandfather, or even your prayer partner when you're backed against the wall. Look to your Source! As soon as the going gets tough, most people run to their employers, thinking they can get an increase in salaries or an advance on their wages. However, as Christians, we must know that our employers are not our source. God is our Source.

Philippians 4:19 does not say, my mama will supply, my daddy will supply, or my husband will supply all of my needs. It doesn't say my church will supply or the government will supply all of my needs! It says, *"My God shall supply all your need according to his riches in glory by Christ Jesus."* If you remember who God is, you will not look to the arms of flesh. God might use them, but you won't look to them.

One day when I was a student at Oral Roberts University, I was walking across the campus with tears running down my face; I was having a little pity party. I had found out that the stipend I received as part of my tennis scholarship had ended. I said, "Oh, God, what am I going to do now?" God responded by speaking to my spirit, "I am your Source, but you are looking to the university."

My words, thoughts, and actions proved that I had made the university my source! I immediately repented, saying, "Lord, forgive me. You are right, Father. I have made ORU my source." It had become my source when I planned the whole semester based on the stipend I expected from the university each month. When I repented, God got my eyes off the university and onto Him, where they should have been all the time.

God supernaturally provided for me when I began looking to Him as my Source. My wife and I lived comfortably that entire year. God turned our situation around! I can give you one testimony after another of how God blessed us abundantly when we looked to Him as our Source and not to the arm of flesh.

So you see, there are three things you must remember when you're backed against the wall: who the Devil is, who you are in Christ, and who God is. Doing so is critical to your success against the Devil. If you do, you'll win each time he comes against you.

When you're backed against the wall—

Remember who the Devil is, who you are, and who God is.

Chapter 10

Give

There's no better time to give than when you're backed against the wall. Often, Christians don't like to talk about money and giving. But giving doesn't always have to involve money. When you're backed against the wall, find something to give. Give clothing. Give of your time. Baby-sit someone's children. Wash someone's car. Cook someone's dinner.

Sowing seeds when you're backed against the wall is biblical. Just realize that those seeds often have the ability to spring up immediately. The widow woman, chosen by God to sustain Elijah during famine, sowed seeds of the little food she had and immediately received enough food to sustain her and her son beyond the famine. (See 1 Kings 17:8–16.) God apparently had already dealt with her, but it was her choice whether she would share with the prophet the last of her food or keep it.

Anytime you say, "God, I don't care what You've been dealing with me about, I'm not going to do it," He is not going to slap you down or kill you over it. But you may miss your opportunity for deliverance.

When Elijah got to Zarephath during the famine, he saw this widow out in her yard gathering sticks, and said, "Fetch me some water, and while you are at it, bake me a little cake." (See verses 10–11.)

Sometimes, God may tell you to give when it looks like you can't afford to give anything at all— when everyone around you would probably call you stupid or crazy for giving five more dollars or taking what food you have and giving it away.

When Elijah approached the widow, the first thing that came out of her mouth was something like this: "Well, I do not have much to give at all. In fact, I was just getting ready to gather some sticks. My son and I were going to cook our last meal, and then we were going to die." (See verse 12.)

By the Spirit of God, Elijah told her, "Bake me a piece of bread first." (See verse 13.) He was saying, "When it looks as if you are going to die, give. When it looks as if you are going under, give." Hoarding is one of the worst things you can do when you're backed against the wall. That is not the time to pinch pennies. Things are already tight, so why not give!

Jesus said as much when He watched another poor widow put *"two mites"* (about fifty cents) into the collection box (Mark 12:42). He sat over against the treasury in the temple and observed how people gave. He saw the rich cast in large amounts. Then he saw this widow throw in two little coins. I imagine some of His disciples said, "Wow! Look at those big givers!"

But Jesus said this woman had given more than all of them because the two coins she gave were all she had (vv. 43–44). Those who had given large gifts made no sacrifice because they gave out of their abundance. The widow gave while her back was against the wall. She gave when she didn't have much to give. She gave when the creditors were breathing down her neck. She gave more than all of the wealthy men, comparatively speaking. You had better believe harvest came to that widow, too, just as it did to the widow who fed Elijah.

It would have been great if the Bible writers had followed up on that story, because I guarantee you that she received her harvest. You may wonder how I can be so sure of that. I'm sure, because that's the way God operates. That's His nature.

Before Peter was chosen as a disciple, Jesus borrowed Peter's fishing boat, which He used as a pulpit. Afterward, Jesus told Peter to launch out into the deep. When Peter obeyed, he caught a great multitude of fish. He caught so many fish that he had to have men from a nearby ship come and help haul in the net. The abundance came after Peter and the other fishermen had been out all night and caught nothing. (See Luke 5:3–7.)

Look for Ways to Give

After the flood in Noah's day, God promised that as long as the earth remains, there will be *"seedtime and harvest"* (Genesis 8:22).

Throughout the Bible and Jesus' ministry, we're taught that if we want God to bless us, we need to give Him something with which to work. If we want something multiplied, we need to give Him something to multiply.

When my wife and I didn't have anything to give, we gave anyway. We cut back on our grocery budget to give. You may think you don't have anything to give. Do you still go grocery shopping? You can give to the food ministry. You can go to the poorer side of town and give someone food to eat.

Instead of filling your gas tank, cut out unnecessary driving and put less gas in the tank. Give that extra money to the ministry. Why? Because you're backed against the wall. Because God takes our net earnings and makes them more than enough when we give.

My wife and I have operated that way all of our married life. From the time we received knowledge of giving and receiving, we acted on those principles. God has multiplied our seed over and over and over again, sometimes immediately.

You can give your way out of bad situations. There is no such thing as not having anything to give. If all you have to give are clothes from your closet, give them, and God will multiply the seed you've sown.

Getting out of Famine

Cast thy bread upon the waters: for thou shalt find it after many days. Give a portion to

seven, and also to eight; for thou knowest not what evil shall be upon the earth.
                                                    (Ecclesiastes 11:1–2)

When you cast your bread on the water (give to God), God says that it will come back to you, although it might take many days. In other words, live a life of giving.

The writer of Ecclesiastes wrote:

If the clouds be full of rain, they empty them-selves upon the earth: and if the tree fall to-wards the south, or toward the north, in the place where the tree falleth, there it shall be. He that observeth the wind shall not sow; and he that regardeth the clouds shall not reap.
                                                    (Ecclesiastes 11:3–4)

This means that if you observe how bad your situation is, you will not sow. It means that if you are walking by your feelings and emotions, you will not give. It's called walking by sight, not by faith. Faith in God is doing what He says, regardless of what we see, think, or feel.

That's why we have to walk according to the Word of God. *"We walk by faith, not by sight"* (2 Corinthians 5:7), and when things get tight, we give to God and begin to bless others.

When things get rough and finances are short, those who walk by faith say, "This is the time to sow. This is the time when I have to sacrifice, the time when I have to give more than I have given in the past. This is a time when I have to go beyond what I have done in the past, beyond what I see or observe with my physical eyes. I command my finances to totally turn around."

He who observes the wind will not sow, and he who looks at the clouds will not reap (Ecclesiastes 11:4). So you have to sow regardless of what the situation looks like. When you're backed against the wall, expect the Devil to pressure you not to give. He'll try to convince you that you can't afford to give, that the timing is wrong for giving, or that you need to borrow money. That's when you must be determined not to count your life dear to yourself; instead, give your way out of your deficit.

God will bless you every time you do this, not just every now and then. I remember people bringing my family groceries, putting money under our door, buying clothes for us, and doing all kinds of unexpected favors. People bought toys and gifts for our children when we couldn't afford to do so. We literally saw God confirm this principle in our lives. And He'll do it for you as well. I challenge you to trust God.

When you're backed against the wall—

Give!

Chapter 11

Associate with Winners

When you're backed against the wall, make sure you spend time around winners. Your ability to selectively choose your associates is crucial. You must associate with people who love God, who talk about the things of God, and who are going places for God.

People who are going places for God don't believe in losing, but in winning. They talk victory, they walk victoriously, and they keep smiles on their faces. They talk joy and success all the time. You must associate with people who came out victoriously when their backs were against the wall.

Although God had chosen David to be king of Israel, Saul remained in the king's palace, taunting David for years. But David surrounded himself with winners as he fled from place to place to escape Saul's sword. David's back was against the wall for a long time before he was crowned king.

These be the names of the mighty men whom David had: the Tachmonite that sat in the seat, chief among the captains; the same was Adino the Eznite: he lift up his spear against

*eight hundred, whom he slew at one time.
And after him was Eleazar the son of Dodo
the Ahohite, one of the three mighty men with
David, when they defied the Philistines that
were there gathered together to battle, and
the men of Israel were gone away: he arose,
and smote the Philistines until his hand was
weary, and his hand clave unto the sword:
and the LORD wrought a great victory that
day; and the people returned after him only
to spoil. And after him was Shammah the son
of Agee the Hararite. And the Philistines were
gathered together into a troop, where was a
piece of ground full of lentiles: and the people fled from the Philistines. But he stood in
the midst of the ground, and defended it, and
slew the Philistines: and the LORD wrought a
great victory.* (2 Samuel 23:8–12)

Notice the kind of men David had around him.
With what kind of men and women are you asso-
ciated? You must surround yourself with mighty
men and women of God. Too many Christians are
running around with Mickey Mouses and acting
like them. We need to spend time with super men
and women of faith.

If my back is against the wall, I want to run
around with someone who says, "Now, listen; you
can lick this thing. I took a spear and killed eight
hundred men one time. If I can do that, so can
you." That kind of pep talk is going to fire me up.
It's going to strengthen my emotions.

If you are going to win, you are going to have
to evaluate the company you keep. I don't care

how long you have been friends with them. You have to ask yourself sometimes, "Has this person ever succeeded at anything? Has he or she ever done anything for God? Does he set goals and accomplish things in life?" If not, there's no benefit to your being around the person, especially now. The only direction he would take you in would be backward.

If you're not moving forward, you are going backward. Even when it appears you're standing still, you're actually going backward or forward. There is no such thing as a standstill in your life in the natural or in the spirit realm.

If you are not going forward in your faith, your finances, your marriage, and your relationship with your children, you are going backward. Although things may appear the same, in the spirit realm something is taking place that you eventually will see with your physical eyes, which could set you back or could take you forward.

Don't be deceived because the situation doesn't appear to have changed. Things happening in the realm of the spirit will either bless your situation or worsen it.

It's crucial for churches to place the right kind of people in leadership positions because pastors are affected by the kind of people surrounding them. At one church I pastored, I had a board of stewardesses that was full of strife and contention. I had to replace its members because it seemed they allowed the Devil to control them.

I appointed a brand-new board, whose members were full of Jesus, full of the Holy Spirit, and ready to walk in love and flow with the pastor. That made a difference for me, the ministry, and the church.

Pastors, as well as people who have their backs against the wall, need to be surrounded by the kind of men David had around him. He had men who said, "We will fight until our hands get weary, until our hands get stuck on the sword." They stood by David in trouble, and it was obvious that they loved him, because of what they did when he happened to mention something that he really craved.

> *And three of the thirty chief went down, and came to David in the harvest time unto the cave of Adullam: and the troop of the Philistines pitched in the valley of Rephaim. And David was then in an hold, and the garrison of the Philistines was then in Bethlehem. And David longed, and said, Oh that one would give me drink of the water of the well of Bethlehem, which is by the gate! And the three mighty men brake through the host of the Philistines, and drew water out of the well of Bethlehem, that was by the gate, and took it, and brought it to David: nevertheless he would not drink thereof, but poured it out unto the LORD. And he said, Be it far from me, O LORD, that I should do this: is not this the blood of the men that went in jeopardy of their lives? therefore he would not drink it. These things did these three mighty men.*
>
> (2 Samuel 23:13–17)

Those three mighty men were not afraid of the Philistines. They were not afraid of trouble, nor were they afraid of obstacles or difficult circumstances.

> *And Abishai, the brother of Joab, the son of Zeruiah, was chief among three. And he lifted up his spear against three hundred, and slew them, and had the name among three. Was he not most honourable of three? therefore he was their captain: howbeit he attained not unto the first three. And Benaiah the son of Jehoiada, the son of a valiant man, of Kabzeel, who had done many acts, he slew two lionlike men of Moab: he went down also and slew a lion in the midst of a pit in time of snow: and he slew an Egyptian, a goodly man: and the Egyptian had a spear in his hand; but he went down to him with a staff, and plucked the spear out of the Egyptian's hand, and slew him with his own spear.*
>
> (2 Samuel 23:18–21)

Do you see the kind of men David surrounded himself with? No wonder he was a great king! No wonder he was a great man. Those around him helped him to be great.

You are not great by yourself. People help you to be great. Those you run around with help you to become great. It's our responsibility to choose the associations that propel and challenge us to greatness. Iron sharpens iron (Proverbs 27:17).

When you're backed against the wall—

Associate with winners.

Chapter 12

Fast and Pray

What better time to fast and pray than when you're backed against the wall? Fasting without prayer has no spiritual benefit. The whole idea of fasting is to get closer to God. What is the point of getting closer to God if you are not talking to Him and listening to His responses? Fasting without prayer is like trying to walk on one leg. Likewise, the church today needs to understand that prayer without fasting also limits Christians' spiritual growth. Because I have talked about prayer throughout this book, most of this chapter concentrates on fasting.

When was the last time you fasted? When was the last time you went without a meal on purpose? Jesus, our primary Example, fasted, and He said that His disciples would fast after He was gone. He didn't say they might or should, but that they would. Actually, He put it this way when He was confronted by the disciples of John the Baptist about why His disciples did not fast as they and the Pharisees did:

> *And Jesus said unto them, Can the children of the bridechamber mourn, as long as the bridegroom is with them? but the days will*

come, when the bridegroom shall be taken
from them, and then shall they fast.
(Matthew 9:15)

Notice that Jesus said His disciples would fast
after He returned to heaven. In Matthew 6:16, He
said, *"When ye fast."* Jesus took for granted that
His people would fast. He said *"when,"* not *if* you
fast.

Moreover, when ye fast, be not, as the hypo-
crites, of a sad countenance: for they disfig-
ure their faces, that they may appear unto
men to fast. Verily I say unto you, They have
their reward. But thou, when thou fastest,
anoint thine head, and wash thy face: that
thou appear not unto men to fast, but unto thy
Father which is in secret: and thy Father,
which seeth in secret, shall reward thee
openly. (Matthew 6:16–18)

Jesus said *"when"* you fast. Now that means He
expects us to fast. He must have expected us to be
disciplined in the area of fasting. The early Christians included fasting as part of their spiritual
walk. However, from about the fourth century until
the Reformation, fasting had degenerated into religious rituals just as it was for the Jews in Jesus'
day.

There are spiritual benefits of fasting if un-
dertaken with the right attitudes. In Matthew 6,
Jesus preached against fasting with the wrong attitudes. He certainly was not preaching against
fasting itself, but against doing it religiously or

hypocritically for people to see how spiritual you supposedly are.

However, don't think fasting twists God's arm, because it doesn't. Fasting will not make God do anything. But there are definite benefits to fasting. Fasting changes you and helps stop the Devil's work in your life. You position yourself where things can happen, where you can receive from God to help get your back off the wall. When you are not focused on the body, you can focus more on spiritual things. Fasting helps you to become sensitive to your spirit. Man is a three-part be-ing—spirit, soul, and body. (See 1 Thessalonians 5:23.)

Two Kinds of Fasting

There are two categories of fasting: a pro-claimed corporate fast, which is for a congrega-tion, nation, or collective body; and a personal fast for individuals.

Within these two categories are various kinds of fasts: a total fast, which means only water is consumed; a liquid fast, which means no solid food is eaten for a specified period of time; and a "no pleasant food" fast, which means denying your body those foods it really likes.

Fasting is important to the believer, and it should be a part of our Christian walk. When you're backed against the wall, it's a good time to fast. In the Bible, whenever God's people had their backs against the wall, if they proclaimed a fast and sincerely sought God's face in the midst of that fast, deliverance came.

Corporate Fast

King Jehoshaphat called a fast because the enemy was talking about coming against his people, and he didn't know what to do. He became afraid, but he proclaimed a corporate fast, and deliverance came. (See 2 Chronicles 20:1–29.)

We find another proclaimed corporate fast in the book of Ezra.

> *Then I proclaimed a fast there, at the river of Ahava, that we might afflict ourselves before our God, to seek of him a right way for us, and for our little ones, and for all our substance.* (Ezra 8:21)

So Ezra proclaimed a corporate fast in order to find out the right way. He and approximately two thousand people were traveling from Babylon back to the land of Judah after seventy years of exile. Notice the reason his back was against the wall.

> *For I was ashamed to require of the king a band of soldiers and horsemen to help us against the enemy in the way: because we had spoken unto the king, saying, The hand of our God is upon all them for good that seek him; but his power and his wrath is against all them that forsake him.* (Ezra 8:22)

The "right way" in this case was literal. Ezra wanted God to show them the route to take to avoid robbers and other difficulties. By witnessing to the king about God, he had put them in a position of not being able to ask for soldiers to accompany them to Jerusalem.

If my back is against the wall, I surely want to know the right way for me at that time. I don't want to walk in ignorance and darkness. I would want to find out from God the right way for me right now.

Sometimes, like Ezra, your back may be against the wall because of your taking a stand in faith for the Lord. The apostles all had to deal with those situations, as have millions of Christians over the past two millennia. Certainly, in that case, you should have faith to lean on God and not the world.

Ezra was ashamed to lean on the arm of flesh after he had witnessed to the king that God would take care of them, and he was right. One of the first questions that will come to your mind, whether you are in poor health, dangerous circumstances, or financial despair, is Who can I consult for help?

Ezra said, "We have already made a declaration to the world that the hand of God is upon us for good. And if I have to seek the way of the world, I would be ashamed, because that would be contrary to the declaration of faith that I have made. That would be a negative reflection on God Almighty."

Ezra knew that God expected His people to keep their word, and I imagine he began speaking to himself in this manner: "I am going to have to stick to the words that I declared. Right now, my back is against the wall. I could go to the king, but I said some words that I am not going to change. Instead, I am going to seek God. I am going to fast about this thing."

Ezra's words became a bit in his mouth. He disciplined himself to shut down his system and to stop eating, to deny himself, and to seek the face of God, and so did the other people who were to journey with him. This was a corporate fast—a fast by a group of people. Guess what happened? God answered.

> *Then we departed from the river of Ahava on the twelfth day of the first month, to go unto Jerusalem: and the hand of our God was upon us, and he delivered us from the hand of the enemy, and of such as lay in wait by the way.* (Ezra 8:31)

Through the Bible, when people sought the face of God through fasting and prayer, God answered.

The Personal Fast

The prophet Daniel gave us a good example of the personal fast. He was an individual who fasted and saw results. Daniel 10:3 says that Daniel sought God and denied himself *"pleasant bread."* In other words, this was not a total water fast, but a fasting of foods that he liked.

Daniel needed answers, and an angel came with answers. There are several examples of individual fasts in the book of Daniel.

Fasting Is Important

I believe fasting should become a regular part of our lifestyles as believers. I am for deliverance, and I am for revelation knowledge. I'm in favor of making my spirit-man strong, and fasting helps your spirit-man become strong. Why? Because it shuts down your flesh. The Bible says in Proverbs 4:23 that out of the heart of man (the spirit) flow *"the issues of life."* Your spirit is supposed to sustain you in the day of adversity. As you fast and seek God's face, your flesh takes a backseat to your spirit. Then your spirit can sustain you through adversity.

When your spirit is strong, Ephesians 3:20 can go into operation. That verse gives us the promise that God is *"able to do exceeding abundantly above all that we ask or think, according to the power that worketh in us."* While you are fasting and seeking God's face, praying in tongues, and feeding on the Word of God, your spirit-man strengthens, and you stir up the forces of God inside you.

By the power that works in you, things happen far beyond anything that you could ever ask or think. You start thinking words of might, strength, force, and power. Your words are not feeble, weak, or impotent after a fast. You become more like Jesus, who walked in the power of the Spirit after fasting.

Did you ever notice in Matthew 4:11 that after Jesus fasted, angels came and ministered to Him? You can expect the angelic host to work on your behalf and minister on your behalf. Angels getting involved and ministering to me, helping me, and strengthening me would sound awfully good if my back were against the wall.

It may be harder to fast today than in previous eras, because our society is food-crazy. But we can't get caught up in that. I like eating as much as anyone, maybe more than some, but I cannot eat when it is time to fast.

Out of your spirit come the force of faith, the force of righteousness, and the healing power of God. Remember that virtue came out of Jesus when the woman with the issue of blood touched His garment. (See Matthew 9:20–22.)

Fasting also will help you to become more humble. When you sacrifice food for time with God, you are humbling yourself before Him. Also, you are training and disciplining your body, and everyone can use more discipline. You need to be able to push that plate and other things away from you when you're backed against the wall. Fasting fosters humility and discipline.

Biblical Rewards of Fasting

Isaiah 58 is considered the fasting chapter. There God spoke through the prophet what He considers the right kind of fast and listed some of the benefits.

Is not this the fast that I have chosen? to loose the bands of wickedness, to undo the heavy burdens, and to let the oppressed go free, and that ye break every yoke? Is it not to deal thy bread to the hungry, and that thou bring the poor that are cast out to thy house? when thou seest the naked, that thou cover him;

91

> *and that thou hide not thyself from thine own*
> *flesh?* (Isaiah 58:6–7)

God spoke through the prophet about Israelites who lived immorally and unrighteously but
thought that God should answer their prayers because they fasted and kept the religious ordinances. (See Isaiah 58:1–5.) In other words,
fasting is useless if you do it to make up for
cheating, stealing, or bitterness toward other
people.

However, if you care about your fellowmen,
live uprightly before God, feed the hungry, and
share what you have with those who have nothing,
then your fasts will have benefits. In verses 8–12,
some of these benefits are listed:

- Your health will *"spring forth speedily"* (v. 8).
  That is a benefit all of us are interested in having!
- Your righteousness will go before you (v. 8).
  You will be known for your good deeds; your
  good name, or reputation, will pave your way
  with others.
- Your *"rear guard"* will be God Himself (v. 8,
  NKJV). In other words, He will protect you. You
  will call, and the Lord will answer. You will
  cry, and He will say, *"Here I am"* (v. 9). This
  promise applies to every area in which deliverance is needed—mental, financial, physical,
  and emotional.
- The Lord will guide you (v. 11). The Lord will
  not only protect you, but also guide you. And
  Isaiah did not say that God will guide you one

time, but *"continually."* He will bless you so much that you can bless others. The Lord will guide you continually and will satisfy your soul in drought, and He will make your bones fat (v. 11). As a result, you will be *"like a watered garden, and like a spring of water, whose waters fail not"* (v. 11). That means that you will always have an abundance and be able to bless others.

- You will *"ride upon the high places of the earth"* (v. 14). You will be promoted by God and respected by others.

But notice that these promises come only to the one who fasts, and even then, they are only to the one who fasts with his life in order and his heart right toward God. The promises are not made to the person who fasts for show or who thinks fasting can cause God to overlook sinful actions or attitudes.

Do you know that every time your stomach growls, you do not have to eat? It doesn't mean you are hungry. There really is no need for food when your stomach growls. There may be a desire, but not a need.

For those who have never fasted, let me give you a word of warning: Start by fasting one meal. Do not begin by trying to fast a whole week! Just start off with one meal. If you have fasted before, then you know you can go two meals, a whole day, or even longer. But don't jump into fasting three or four days if you have never fasted. That's like trying to lift three hundred pounds when you can't lift fifty pounds. If you are on medication or under a doctor's care, seek the advice of your physician.

You can fast to the point where your body says you cannot go any further. You have lived off the fat and all the stored nutrients in your body, and now you have to eat.

Jesus fasted forty days, and then He was hungry. I am not advocating that anyone fast twenty, thirty, or forty days without being instructed by the Lord to do that and without working up to it. But nearly everyone can go a day without eating. Fasting was important to those who lived in Bible days, and it was important to the early church. I believe it is just as important to us today.

Teaching Children to Fast

I believe we need to start teaching our children how to fast, as well as how to pray and believe God in faith for their needs to be met. From time to time, you should tell your children, "Today, you are not going to eat lunch. Nobody in the house is, and you are going to find that you can make it until dinner time."

This will begin to encourage them not only in spiritual discipline but also in physical discipline. This will also help you parents in those situations when you are traveling, out shopping, or too busy to prepare a meal right away. There are times when children say they are hungry, and you don't have time to stop. Then you can say, "You have done it before. You know you can make it. You can wait until we are able to prepare a meal."

Our children need to learn to fast while they are young. Of course, you cannot begin teaching them to fast when they are too young, but you can start when they are eight or nine years old. A wise parent knows when his or her children are ready to learn new things. You can teach them spiritual laws, but one thing is for sure: you had better live your faith yourself in front of them! When their backs are against the wall as they become adults, they will know from your example what to do.

Fasting and praying are an important steps in gaining victory in times of tribulation and crises. Pray and fast, and you will find your Christian walk becoming much stronger. Also, I strongly suggest that Isaiah 58 becomes the guideline of fasting for your life.

Like anything with God, fasting must be done in faith. So before beginning your time of fasting and prayer, be specific with God about the reason for the fast, and according to Mark 11:23–24, believe that you receive. That's right. Enter the fast already thanking God for hearing and answering you.

When you're backed against the wall—

Fast and pray.

Chapter 13

Judge Yourself

When you're backed against the wall, you will need to judge yourself. The Greek translation for *judge* in the *King James Version* is *krino,* which means to distinguish or to decide.

When the word *judge* is used in the Bible, it clearly indicates that we are to distinguish, discern, or decide based on God's Word. Only God has the right to judge in the sense of trying and condemning. That's why there seems to be a contradiction when the Bible tells us to examine ourselves on one hand (see 1 Corinthians 11:28) but to *"judge not, that ye be not judged"* (Matthew 7:1) on the other. Judging has two completely different meanings.

Luke 6:35–36 tells us to be merciful to other people, and not to judge and condemn them. The reason is that we will be judged based on the way we judge others (Matthew 7:2). As we forgive, we are forgiven (Matthew 6:12).

Righteous Judgment

There is such a thing as righteous judgment, where a person's lifestyle is measured against the

Word of God. That involves distinguishing right from wrong and deciding that someone or something is not in line with God's Word.

Righteous judgment allows you to identify a person as an alcoholic, a whoremonger, a liar, an adulterer, or whatever the case might be, without condemning the person. Instead, we should love the person and hate the sin in his or her life.

Do not judge people based on hearsay. Righteous judgment is measuring knowledge against the Word of God without being hypocritical, judgmental, or condemning. The same applies when judging yourself.

In 1 Corinthians 11:28, Paul wrote about taking Communion: *"But let a man examine himself, and so let him eat of that bread, and drink of that cup."* Paul said to examine yourself—not to condemn and sentence yourself—so that you can eat and drink of that bread and cup worthily. Verse 29 explains the consequences of eating and drinking unworthily: *"For he that eateth and drinketh unworthily, eateth and drinketh damnation to himself, not discerning the Lord's body."*

Notice that if you eat and drink unworthily, you bring damnation to yourself. *"Unworthily"* means while being in a state of spiritual or carnal sin. In those verses, Paul went on to tie the word *unworthily* to our attitudes toward our brothers and sisters in Christ. So it is important that we examine ourselves.

The damnation Paul referred to may come in the form of problems or hardships. He said, *"For this cause many are weak and sickly among you, and many sleep"* (1 Corinthians 11:30). In other words, many were weak and died prematurely because they took Communion without judging or examining themselves. They brought trouble to themselves through their sins, their self-righteousness, and their judgmental attitudes.

You are being self-righteous when you put yourself in God's place and judge another person. Now, I don't know about you, but the last thing I want to do is to bring problems on myself! That's why I follow Paul's advice and examine myself.

If there's something wrong in your life, the Holy Spirit will show you. You don't have to go on examining yourself for months; nor do you have to worry and fret, thinking there is something wrong with you all of the time.

Self-righteousness Is Pharisaism

Remember the story Jesus told of two men praying in the temple? A Pharisee, observing a tax collector standing across the room, prayed, *"God, I thank thee, that I am not as other men are, extortioners, unjust, adulterers, or even as this publican. I fast twice in the week, I give tithes of all that I possess"* (Luke 18:11–12). On the other hand, the tax collector prayed, *"God be merciful to me a sinner"* (v. 13).

Which prayer do you think was more acceptable to God? If you chose the second one, you were right. Jesus said that man went home justified, rather than the Pharisee: *"For every one that exalteth himself shall be abased; and he that humbleth himself shall be exalted"* (v. 14).

I wonder how many Christians have done that. I wonder how many have consciously or subconsciously thanked God that they were not like Sister or Brother So-and-So. I wonder how many of us are so accustomed to putting down other people that we don't even realize we are measuring them against ourselves or our standards, and not God's.

The Pharisees were meticulous about keeping the laws in case they inadvertently sinned. Yet they were usually full of sin, which was reflected in their self-righteous attitudes and their judgment of other people's behavior.

Jesus told His followers to do what the Pharisees said, because they were the religious leaders, but not to do what they did, because they were hypocrites. (See Matthew 23:3–33.) It's important for you not to slip into the legalistic attitudes of the Pharisees. Legalism will make you sick, rather than help you get away from the wall.

One reason the prophet Daniel remained honorable and respected all his life was that he remained humble. Even in exile and under royal regimes, he stayed humble. He never exalted himself—only God. When praying for the Jewish people, he repented of his sins right along with them. (See Daniel 9:3–19.)

First, examine yourself before you even think about looking at someone else. Jesus is the One who said, *"Judge not, that ye be not judged"* (Matthew 7:1). That does not mean that we don't make assessments and that we don't make decisions about individuals. It does mean that those decisions and assessments must be based on the Word of God, not on what we think.

Poor Financial Decisions

Many of the problems people face are self-imposed. For example, when you're backed against the wall in a financial dilemma, examine yourself to determine if your spending and buying have become out of control. Ask yourself these questions:

- Does a sale cause me to go wild with credit cards?
- Do I feel I have to buy everything I want?
- Do I make bad investment decisions?
- Do I buy nonessentials first, causing bills to go unpaid?
- Do I spend without making out a budget?
- Do I gamble, drink, or smoke, wasting my income in these ways? (Some people are addicted to playing lotteries, bingo, and slot machines, but they don't realize that they are gambling because they're not betting on races, sports, or poker games.)
- Do I withhold tithes and offerings to the Lord?
- Do I ignore the plight of the poor and needy? (John wrote in 1 John 3:17 that the one who ignores the poor does not have the love of God in him.)
- Do I have the love of God in me?

But whoso hath this world's good, and seeth his brother have need, and shutteth up his bowels of compassion from him, how dwelleth the love of God in him? (1 John 3:17)

Bad decision-making and bad budgeting are among the reasons people find themselves against the wall. I'm sure, like me, you would never want to bring problems on yourself.

If I examine myself and find that I am the source of my problems, I immediately begin to straighten things out. Proverbs 26:2 says, *"As the bird by wandering, as the swallow by flying, so the curse causeless ["a curse without cause,"* NKJV] *shall not come."*

Examine Yourself for Pride

If we find our backs against the wall, pride is the first of three spiritual areas for which we need to examine ourselves.

I wonder how many of us realize that every time we put down someone else, we are lifting up ourselves. There's an old saying that when you point a finger at someone else, three fingers are pointing back toward you. It's time for us to humble ourselves. What do we have anyway that God did not give us? Pride will hurt and even kill us.

Pride is more than being conceited or arrogant. Pride is thinking more highly of yourself than you ought to think (see Romans 12:3); thinking you are hot stuff—God's gift to women or God's gift to men; thinking that you know everything, and that no one can tell you anything.

God wants us to stay teachable. Pride hurts us every time. God resists the proud and gives grace to the humble (James 4:6). He will exalt the humble and abase the proud (Job 40:11). Abase means to bring low. God is saying, "Your pride will cause Me to take My hands off you and allow the Enemy to come upon you." Pride brings all kinds of turmoil and devastation.

Saul, the first king of Israel, fell into pride after he became established on the throne. And Samuel, the prophet who anointed him king, finally had to say to him, *"When thou wast little in thine own sight, wast thou not made the head of the tribes of Israel, and the LORD anointed thee king over Israel?"* (1 Samuel 15:17).

Samuel was saying to Saul, "When you thought little of yourself, when you were teachable, when you were open for constructive criticism, when you thought you didn't even deserve a position, that's when God promoted you. Now you think so highly of yourself that you are even in rebellion against God Himself!"

Pride Will Destroy You

There was a king in the New Testament, named Herod, who got into trouble for exalting himself as a god. As he was giving a speech, some residents of Tyre and Sidon tried to gain Herod's favor by praising him, saying, *"It is the voice of a god, and not of a man"* (Acts 12:22). The Bible states in the next verse: *"And immediately the angel of the Lord smote him, because he gave not God the glory: and he was eaten of worms, and gave up the ghost."* Herod was smitten not for his natural sins, but for his spiritual sin of pride.

We must not be high-minded. Pastors and others in the ministry are not immune to pride. We must not consider ourselves mighty men and women of faith who have nothing to learn from anyone else. Any person who begins to think he or she knows it all is on his or her way to destruction. Pride will get your back against the wall very quickly.

God Hates Pride

It would be good for you to look up all of the Scriptures in the Bible that refer to pride and to proud people, but here are two to consider:

Every one that is proud in heart is an abomination to the LORD: though hand join in hand, he shall not be unpunished. (Proverbs 16:5)

Pride goeth before destruction, and an haughty spirit before a fall. (Proverbs 16:18)

Pride causes you never to say, "I am sorry. It's my fault." Pride always blames someone else by saying, "No, it wasn't my fault," or "This would never have happened if it hadn't been for what you did."

There are all kinds of ways to recognize pride. When you're backed against the wall, you ought to get before God and start looking at yourself. Ask yourself: "Have I been walking in pride? Have I been putting people down? Do I think I am better than other people and find myself resenting someone else's suggestions? Have I closed myself off to the point where I can no longer receive instruction?"

103

Pride has its own revelation. However, any revelation outside of the Word of God is destructive, and pride will cause you not to listen to others. The Bible says that in a multitude of counselors, there is safety (Proverbs 11:14). When you don't want to listen to others, you are on your way down. When you're at the point where no one can tell you anything, you are on your way down. Paul said that you should think good and highly of yourself, but not more highly than you ought to think. (See Romans 12:3.)

In Proverbs 6:16–19, God told us seven things He hates. He feels so strongly about these seven things that He called them abominations. The first thing He named was a proud look.

As Daniel, David, Abraham, Isaac, and Paul stayed humble, I want to stay humble. I can use the mercies of God every day, and I thank Him that they are new every morning. (See Lamentations 3:22–23.) We will never come to a point where we don't need the mercy of God.

Pride puts a wall between you and others. It breaks the unity that God wants for the body of Christ. (See 1 Corinthians 12:25–27.) Pride keeps people from fitting into the body where God has chosen for them to fit. It causes fingers to want to be mouths and hands to want to be feet. (See 1 Corinthians 12:15–20.) Stay free of pride.

Unforgiveness

The second area in which to examine yourself is in the area of unforgiveness. Are you holding grudges against someone? With whom are you not speaking? Who are you rolling your eyes at? Whose name has been scratched off your list?

Jesus said if you are holding anything against others, forgive them, so *"that your Father also which is in heaven may forgive you your trespasses"* (Mark 11:25). In other words, if you hold things against others, the Devil will chase you and beat you all over the place. Personally, I don't like the Devil beating up on me; therefore, I endeavor to forgive quickly.

Hebrews 12:15 talks about a *"root of bitterness"* that affects not only your life, but also the lives of those with whom you come in contact. That bitter root is unforgiveness: "Looking diligently lest any man fail of the grace of God; lest any root of bitterness springing up trouble you, and thereby many be defiled."

Your unforgiveness of one or both of your parents can defile your relationship with your spouse and certainly with your children. What you hold against them is tied to you, not to them. Nine times out of ten, you will commit the very offense that you would not forgive them for doing.

How many times have you heard someone say, "When I was little, I swore I would never do that to my children? Yet that is exactly what I am doing." That's why child abuse, for example, seems to be generational. Many of the challenges in our lives stem from our attitudes, words, and actions.

Creating Your Tomorrow with Your Mouth

This last area may seem minor, but it can actually leave us vulnerable by tearing holes in our divine protection. Recently, I heard someone console a person by saying, "I know how you feel." The Spirit of God spoke inside me and said, "You've said that so many times, and you have to stop saying it."

You may say that's such a little thing. That's just being polite and showing sympathy. That's simply good manners. That's not true. Every time, I told somebody, "I know how you feel," I was creating my tomorrow.

I could truthfully say, "I've experienced that feeling before," or "That is too bad." You can sympathize with someone without producing a tomorrow for yourself and without reidentifying with a similar situation that caused you pain and sorrow.

It seemed like a minute issue that God dealt with me about. He was showing me that the curses do not come without a reason. A lot of little words have come out of our mouths, creating situations, because the tongue is like the bit that controls the horse and the helm that turns a ship. (See James 3:3–5.) It's especially important to guard your mouth when it comes to your children, your health, your employer, and your job.

Watch what you say, although you have to let other people say what they want to say. No one wants you to be told how to talk, so don't get on someone else's case. Deal with yourself. If you go around trying to be everybody's teacher, you will turn people off. That could rob you of opportunities to tell them about Jesus. And before long, you could go off on an ego trip, particularly if people begin listening to you.

Little Things Mean a Lot

I don't want to sound too harsh or as if I'm majoring on minors. I believe the Lord is saying that we need to grow in stature like Jesus.

Many of the troubles we create could be eliminated if we would examine ourselves periodically and ask the Holy Spirit to correct us. We have enough challenges from other people and attacks from the Enemy without creating adversities for ourselves.

Ask yourself, "Am I walking in pride, unforgiveness, strife, or resentment? Am I harboring bitterness against others? Am I being teachable?"

Examine your attitudes and words, as well as your actions. Determine what you could have done to cause your problems, what your disposition is, how you have conducted yourself, and who you are out to get.

Perhaps nothing in this chapter pertains directly to you. Maybe the Holy Spirit was able to point something else out to you.

For example, judgment came to Eli, the high priest in Samuel's day, because he didn't rule his children properly. (See 1 Samuel 3:11–14.) Have you allowed your children to do whatever they want to do, when they want to do it? Have you allowed them to speak and act any way they wanted? Lack of discipline is not love. Actually, it is as bad for them as the other extreme—abusiveness.

Perhaps you have never struck your children with a stick or belt, but you abuse them verbally or emotionally. The curse does not come without a reason. A spoiled child can reap negative consequences just as easily as an abused one.

What is your relationship like with your wife or husband, your parents, your coworkers, and your friends? We should all examine ourselves for offensiveness, apathy, slothfulness, stubbornness, poor stewardship, and other flaws.

We should look closely at the seven things God hates (Proverbs 6:16–19) to see if any of them are operating in our lives:

- A proud look
- A lying tongue
- Hands that shed innocent blood (This does not have to be literal. It could be assassinating someone's character or killing someone's ministry. Can you imagine how God feels about abortionists? However, let me warn you: He does not need us to carry out judgment on them by execution!)
- Devising wicked imaginations
- Feet that are swift to run to mischief
- Those who give false witness or lie
- Those who sow discord among the brethren, which includes people who start problems in churches

Have you been responsible for starting an undercurrent in the church against the pastor or against certain leaders? Is your heart right toward other people at home, on the job, or in church?

If you're guilty of any of the seven abominations, repent quickly, turn away from them, or let go of that attitude. God is faithful to forgive you, according to 1 John 1:9, and then He will show you a way out of your troubles. (See 1 Corinthians 10:13.)

When you're backed against the wall—

Judge yourself.

Chapter 14

Praise and Worship God

P raise and worship are among your most powerful tools when it seems there is no way out. The Word of God makes a distinction between *praise* and *worship.* When you're backed against the wall, you want to do both, because this is a sure way of deliverance.

What Is Praise?

Praise is an expression of who God is and what He has done. It is declaring to God with your mouth His attributes, who He is, and what He has done. Praise is commending and giving honor to someone.

Praise might go something like this: "Father God, I thank You for Your goodness and Your mercy. I thank You, Lord, for my family. I thank You for healing me of arthritis that was in my left pelvic bone. I thank you for giving me direction in my life. I thank You for helping us build this facility. Lord, I thank You for the healing You have brought to my body over and over again when I was attacked. I thank You for financial blessings. I thank You for your holiness, Your purity, Your strength, Your might."

That's praise. So if praise is thanking God and telling Him how much we appreciate everything He has done, then what is the difference between praise and worship? Simply defined, praise is thanking God for what He has done, and worship is commending God for who He is. We'll discuss worship a little later.

In Matthew 21, after Jesus had chased the money changers out of the temple, people who were blind and lame came to him, and He healed them. The religious officials saw these healings and miracles, and they heard children in the crowd begin to sing praises to Jesus.

And when the chief priests and scribes saw the wonderful things that he did, and the children crying in the temple, and saying, Hosanna to the son of David; they were sore displeased, and said unto him, Hearest thou what these say? And Jesus saith unto them, Yea; have ye never read, Out of the mouth of babes and sucklings thou hast perfected praise? (Matthew 21:15–16)

The Pharisees didn't believe Jesus was the Messiah and certainly not the Son of God. In their minds such claims were blasphemy. However, Jesus was explaining to them that the children were praising Him.

When they cried, *"Hosanna, to the son of David,"* they were worshipping Jesus for who He is—the Messianic Son of God. They were also praising Him for what He had done. Jesus didn't say that, but that's the impression we get from the children's warm reception of His ministry. Based on the children's reaction, the religious leaders should have known who He was.

In Luke 19:37–40, we see another account:

And when he was come nigh, even now at the descent of the mount of Olives, the whole multitude of the disciples began to rejoice and praise God with a loud voice for all the mighty works that they had seen; saying, Blessed be the King that cometh in the name of the Lord: peace in heaven, and glory in the highest. And some of the Pharisees from among the multitude said unto him, Master, rebuke thy disciples. And he answered and said unto them, I tell you that, if these should hold their peace, the stones would immediately cry out.

What would the stones immediately cry out? "Praise! Praise!"

Praise Brings Deliverance

In Acts 16 we see a perfect example of two people in real trouble, a life-and-death situation in which praise and worship brought deliverance. Paul and Silas prayed and sang songs to God at midnight.

Paul and Silas had gotten into trouble for casting out of a servant girl a spirit that allowed her to tell the future. Her masters earned money from her fortune-telling. Those men accused Paul and Silas of causing trouble by teaching customs against Roman tradition, and the multitude dragged them to the magistrates. The judges tore off Paul's and Silas's clothes and had them beaten and thrown into prison. *"And at midnight Paul and Silas prayed, and sang praises unto God: and the prisoners heard them"* (Acts 16:25).

You may think their situation doesn't apply to you. However, "midnight," used figuratively, represents the darkest, most trying time in your life. Midnight is when it seems like all hell has come against you. Let's say, for instance, that you lost your job and you owe everybody. Everything is falling out from under you at the same time, and you do not know how you are going to come out of it.

In their darkest hour, Paul and Silas sang praises to God because they had prayed in faith. Whenever you pray in faith, you can start singing praises.

Faith says, "I know my God heard me."

Faith says, "I know my God will answer me."

Faith says, "I have the answer before I can even see it."

So they possibly prayed along these lines: "Lord, I know You are going to bring us out of this. Your hand is on our lives. You called us to preach to the nations. I know You will never leave us or forsake us. I know You will make a way for us out of this prison. Our work is not done, so we are getting out of here, God. We know it, and we thank You for it." And they began to sing praises.

We see in the next verse how God responded. *"Suddenly there was a great earthquake, so that the foundations of the prison were shaken: and immediately all the doors were opened, and every one's bands were loosed"* (Acts 16:26).

They were free through praise, and I am sure they immediately thanked God. The Bible says,

> *It is a good thing to give thanks unto the* LORD. (Psalm 92:1)

> *By him therefore let us offer the sacrifice of praise to God continually, that is, the fruit of our lips giving thanks to his name*
> (Hebrews 13:15)

> *In every thing give thanks: for this is the will of God in Christ Jesus concerning you.*
> (1 Thessalonians 5:18)

Praise will bring God on the scene.

Praise will bring deliverance to your life.

Praise triggers the power of God on your behalf.

Look at what happened to the city of Jericho when the second-generation Israelites were ready to take the Promised Land. God Himself gave Joshua the strategy for taking Jericho.

"Joshua," He said, "have your people march around the city once a day for six days, and on the seventh day, have them march around the city seven times. On the seventh time, I want the trumpets to sound and the people to shout. And the walls will come down." (See Joshua 6:2–5.)

114

They followed God's instructions, and on the seventh day, they marched around Jericho seven times. On that seventh time, the trumpets blew, and the people began to shout.

I believe they shouted, "Praise the Lord, for He is good! His mercy endures forever."

That phrase, *"His mercy endureth for ever,"* is repeated more than forty times in the Bible, about half of them in the Psalms, which were written as praise and worship songs. God wants us to see the contrast between how long His mercy, truth, goodness, peace, and righteousness last and how long His anger lasts, which is *"but a moment"* (Psalm 30:5).

As the Israelites shouted unto God, the Bible says the walls began to crumble. They seized Jericho through praise and obedience. The ark of the covenant went around that city once a day for six days and seven times on the seventh day.

The ark of the covenant is the Word of God, which is the power of God. The power of God was weakening those walls every day. Therefore, all the Israelites had to do after that was shout and praise God for His goodness. And the walls came down.

Then, we have the example in 2 Chronicles 20 of Jehosaphat of Judah. This king and the people of Judah employed a number of methods we have discussed in this book to get their backs off a very tough-to-escape wall. They had been attacked by a multitude of soldiers from Moab, Ammon, and other Canaanite tribes.

They fasted corporately and prayed. They guarded their minds and reminded themselves of the Word of God. They repented and reminded themselves of who they were and who God is. They sought God for special instructions.

When they cried out to God, He told them to put singers before the army and let them shout praises to God. The soldiers thought they were going to have to fight. But God said, in essence, "All you are going to have to do is praise Me."

They praised and praised and praised! The Bible says that God sent an ambushment, and the enemy began to fight among themselves. Praise brought deliverance. If it brought deliverance then, it will bring deliverance now.

If praising God for deliverance before it happens was a principle back then, it is a principle now. Jesus is always the same, which means God never changes. (See Hebrews 13:8.) Therefore, He will do the same thing now that He did then.

If you will stand up and shout for a while, "Praise the Lord for He is good. His mercy endures forever," God will respond. The Bible says that He inhabits the praises of His people (Psalm 22:3), and praise is to be in the life of every believer.

We need to understand that we are to live in the realm of both praise and worship. Both principles of praise and worship are applicable to our lives.

What Is Worship?

Worship is when a person or a group of people spontaneously and genuinely recognize God for who He is. When we spend time just loving

God the Father, God the Son, and God the Holy
Spirit for being our Creator, Father, Savior,
Healer, and all that He is to us, we are worship-
ping Him.

In many churches, people gather for what
they call worship services; instead, they perform
a series of ritualistic ceremonies. How many times
have you heard people say their church has two
worship services on Sundays? That statement im-
plies that everything that goes on in those services involves worshipping God. However, that's
rarely the case. In a lot of services God is hardly,
if ever, worshipped at all.

When I was in a denominational church, we
often sang a song as part of our religious ritual
that says, "Hear our prayer, O Lord; incline thine
ear to us." One morning, the Spirit of God spoke
inside me and said, "Don't ever sing that song
again." While it may have sounded religious, the
words were faithless because they contradicted
God's Word.

The Bible says that the eyes and ears of the
Lord are open to the righteous (1 Peter 3:12). And
if I pray according to His Word, I know He hears
me. So why would I sing a song that begs God to
hear me? Yet in that church, at that time, singing
that verse was only a ritual, a part of a ceremony
that we called worship.

If we want to praise and worship God, we
must know what real praise and true worship are.
In Matthew 21, we see a classic example of what
praise and worship are not. We also see how God
feels about worship that is not truly worship of
Him.

And Jesus went into the temple of God, and cast out all them that sold and bought in the temple, and overthrew the tables of the moneychangers, and the seats of them that sold doves. And said unto them, It is written, My house shall be called the house of prayer; but ye have made it a den of thieves. And the blind and the lame came to him in the temple; and he healed them. (Matthew 21:12–14)

If Jesus were on earth today and walked into some churches, He would do the same thing. He has not changed. He is not going to change. Just because it's two thousand years later doesn't mean Jesus wouldn't do the same thing. He doesn't ever want His house made into a den of thieves.

There were so many distractions in God's house that people were hindered from learning about God and how to worship Him *"in spirit and in truth"* (John 4:24). The church had fallen prey to a spirit of greed. The caretakers were using it for buying and selling merchandise and for ripping off the poor.

After Jesus threw the money changers out of the temple, immediately, "the blind and the lame" came to Him. That's what church is all about. It's for people to come in order to receive ministry and to get their needs met.

Jesus explains the purpose of worship:

But the hour cometh, and now is, when the true worshippers shall worship the Father in spirit and in truth: for the Father seeketh such

to worship him. God is a Spirit: and they that
worship him must worship him in spirit and in
truth.   (John 4:23–24)

Worship Is of the Spirit

God is looking for those who will worship Him in spirit, and you can't do that until you are first filled with the Spirit. You have to be filled with the Holy Spirit in order to worship God in the spirit. You have to be able to pray in other tongues to worship God in the spirit.

You can't really have true worship when you formulate the words with your intellect, which is part of your flesh. You are a three-part being: spirit, soul (mind, will, and emotions), and body. And God says that the true worshippers will worship from their spirits, not from their soulish realm.

Worship is defined as giving reverence; it is the pressure to release from within you an expression of the awesome feeling toward deity.

Worship also means to make obeisance, which is the gesture or action of bowing or kneeling to someone or something.

That is what God is after—true worshippers, bowing down to Him in spirit and in truth.

Worship Brings Deliverance

Look at the account of the leper coming to Jesus.

And, behold, there came a leper and wor-
shipped him, saying, Lord, if thou wilt, thou

119

*canst make me clean. And Jesus put forth his
hand, and touched him, saying, I will, be thou
clean. And immediately his leprosy was
cleansed.* (Matthew 8:2–3)

We have the accounts of the Syrophenician
woman whose daughter was grievously vexed
with a devil. The woman came and fell at the feet
of Jesus, worshipping Him and calling Him the Son
of David, a Messianic term, and saying, "Lord,
help me." When the woman returned to her
house, she found that the demon had gone out of
her daughter. (See Matthew 15:22–28; Mark 7:25–
30.)

We have a similar account in Matthew 9:18.
The ruler of a synagogue came and worshipped
Jesus, saying that his daughter was *"even now
dead: but come and lay* [Your] *hand upon her, and
she shall live."* Jesus went in to the young girl, took
her by the hand, and raised her from the dead.

In each of these accounts the person fell at Jesus' feet and worshipped Him. And in each account, there was deliverance. When our backs are
against the wall, we need to worship—to fall down
at Jesus' feet, bow down before God, and express
praise for who God is: "Father, You are the Creator of heaven and earth, and there is no God like
You. You made all that is in the world, the sea, and
the heavens."

If we begin to live a lifestyle of praise and
worship, it will bring deliverance to our lives over
and over again. Murmuring, complaining, bick-
ering, and calling everybody to pray for you
won't bring deliverance, but praise and worship

will. Praise and worship bring the blessings and favor of God and allow Him to show Himself strong in our lives.

When you're backed against the wall—

Praise and worship God.

Chapter 15

Change What Needs to Be Changed

When you're backed against the wall, make sure you hold fast to your confession. Watch your mouth, and change what needs to be changed. These two things go hand in hand when you're backed against the wall. You must continue believing and saying what God said and be willing to make whatever changes necessary when things are pointed out to you concerning your situation.

Hold Fast

Hebrews 10:23 says, *"Let us hold fast the profession of our faith without wavering; (for he is faithful that promised)."* To *"hold fast"* means not to let go. Do not let your profession (or confession) go.

Have you ever seen someone ride a roller coaster for the first time? The majority of first-timers will never let go of that rail. They hold on tight. I'm sure if you ever rode a roller coaster and were afraid, you held on tight, clinging to that rail.

Well, that's what God wants us to do. He wants us to cling to our faith and hold on to it tightly!

We are supposed to profess our faith by proclaiming what God says about our situation and circumstances, knowing that by faith it will come to pass. Faith is believing the Word of God. Romans 10:17 says, *"Faith comes by hearing, and hearing by the word of God"* (NKJV). You can't have faith without the Word. The Word is faith, and you are to hold fast the profession of the Word without wavering.

The Devil wants you to waver when you're backed against the wall. To waver means to sometimes go this way and sometimes that way. James described the condition and result of one who wavers:

> *But let him ask in faith, nothing wavering. For he that wavereth is like a wave of the sea driven with the wind and tossed. For let not that man think that he shall receive any thing of the Lord. A double minded man is unstable in all his ways.* (James 1:6–8)

If you are confessing that by Jesus' stripes you are healed, and the doctor tells you he can't do anything else for you and that you have six months to live, you must hold fast to your faith. If you want to be healed, never say what the doctor said. Just keep saying what Jesus did according to 1 Peter 2:24:

> *Who his own self bare our sins in his own body on the tree, that we, being dead to sins,*

should live unto righteousness: by whose stripes ye were healed.

When you get up in the morning and you're not feeling well, start your day by saying and believing, "By Jesus' stripes I was healed two thousand years ago. Therefore, I am already healed today. I believe that I receive."

Don't say anything differently around the clock. If you wake up feeling sick, don't say, "Oh, I'm feeling bad." Instead say, "By His stripes I am healed." Regardless of the circumstances, don't let go of your profession of faith. That's the kind of decision you have to make to win.

The same is true with finances. It doesn't matter what your finances look like. If you are a tither, keep saying, "My God opens the windows of heaven and pours out a blessing for me that I don't have room enough to receive." (See Malachi 3:10.)

Holding Fast Goes against the World's Ways

Think of the Hebrew children—Daniel, Shadrach, Meshach, and Abednego—all from the tribe of Judah. These youth made the decision when being led away into captivity that they would never forsake the Lord their God by worshipping the false gods of Babylon.

The Hebrew children held fast to their professions and won. They would not eat of the Babylonians' delicacies, even though they were roasted in honey and veal and soaked in milk. Instead, they stuck to their diets of fruits, vegetables, and water, and they were healthier and sharper than any of the other captives. God honored the fact that they never wavered regardless of the pressure or circumstances. (See Daniel 1:3–20.)

When King Nebuchadnezzar talked to them, he was impressed by their God-given wisdom and knowledge. Daniel got promoted after reciting and interpreting a dream of Nebuchadnezzar's that no one else had been able to interpret. At Daniel's request, the king ended up promoting Shadrach, Meshach, and Abednego to official positions as well. (See Daniel 2:46–49.)

Hold Fast When the Heat Is On

Sometimes, holding fast to the profession of your faith seems to the world like antisocial or weird behavior. There are times you can expect to be persecuted. (See 2 Timothy 3:12.) However, when you're backed against the wall for the Lord's sake, you can expect Him to come through to defend His Word.

Nebuchadnezzar made the decree that everyone in his kingdom must bow down to a golden image he had created to worship. Well, Shadrach, Meshach, and Abednego decided beforehand that they would serve no other gods, because there is no other God, except Jehovah. Although Nebuchadnezzar promoted them in the natural, they knew it was God who was really behind it all. They were holding tight to their profession of faith without wavering.

Soon word of their rebellion reached the king. Nebuchadnezzar became furious, and in his rage and fury, he commanded the three Hebrews to bow down when the musicians played; otherwise, they would suffer the consequence! They would be thrown into a furnace that would be heated seven times hotter than what it normally was.

Shadrach, Meshach, and Abednego were not intimidated by the circumstances and replied,

If it be so, our God whom we serve is able to deliver us from the burning fiery furnace, and he will deliver us out of thine hand, O king. But if not, be it known unto thee, O king, that we will not serve thy gods, nor worship the golden image which thou hast set up.
(Daniel 3:17–18)

They said, "Listen, king; you can make it hotter if you want to, but we are not going to bow. And not only that, if you throw us in, we are not going to burn!" Their minds were made up. They held fast to their profession of faith. They made that kind of decision when they were being taken into bondage. Then, when the heat came on them, literally and figuratively, they held fast to their profession.

They didn't say, "Oh, we'll bow now! Oh, we never knew our lives would be put on the line like this! We'll bow." They didn't bow, and they won a great victory. They have a testimony that thousands of years later is still blessing people's lives and encouraging others to hold fast to the profession of their faith without wavering.

We may not experience persecution to the extent that they did, but whatever we go through, we must not let go of our profession of faith. It doesn't matter if you get laid off your job. Don't start saying that you don't know how you are going to make it. Begin to say, "I have already made it because I have been delivered from the powers of darkness and translated into the kingdom of God's dear Son."

Never say that you don't know how you are going to make it. God already made the way for you to make it. You just haven't tapped into it yet. But as you serve God and hold fast to your profession, you are going to tap into His plan for your life, along with His wisdom and His strength.

In Hebrews 4:14–17 we read,

> *Seeing then that we have a great high priest, that is passed into the heavens, Jesus the Son of God, let us hold fast our profession. For we have not an high priest which cannot be touched with the feeling of our infirmities; but was in all points tempted like as we are, yet without sin. Let us therefore come boldly unto the throne of grace, that we may obtain mercy, and find grace to help in time of need.*

We can get strength, obtain mercy, and find grace when our backs are against the wall, if we hold fast to our profession of faith and keep looking to Jesus. Never stop saying what God says. When the heat is on, my friend, continue saying what God says.

Say what God says when everything is going well—and when things aren't going so well, too.

Everything you see is temporary and subject to change. In fact, everything is always in the process of changing.

We are winners today and *"more than conquerors"* (Romans 8:37). We are *"the head, and not the tail;...above only, and...not...beneath"* (Deuteronomy 28:13).

The key to the quality of your life is in your mouth. Death and life are in the words of your mouth. (See Proverbs 18:21.) In fact, Solomon wrote: *"A wholesome tongue is a tree of life"* (Proverbs 15:4), and *"A man's belly shall be satisfied with the fruit of his mouth"* (Proverbs 18:20).

Matthew 12:37 tells us that we will be *"justified"* and *"condemned"* by the words of our mouths. James said that blessing and cursing should not come out of the same mouth any more than sweet and bitter water should come out of the same fountain (James 3:10–11).

Make sure the words you speak are always sweet. If you want sweet words, speak the Word of God, which is *"sweeter also than honey and the honeycomb"* (Psalm 19:10), and of more value than silver and gold (Psalm 119:72).

Don't Murmur and Complain

If you are an heir of God and a joint-heir with Christ, don't grumble or complain. Instead of telling others how bad things are, tell them what Jesus has done for you and will do for you. What good is it to go around telling people about your hardships and how people are mistreating and misunderstanding you?

Your job is to demonstrate that you have overcome by the blood of the Lamb and the word of your testimony (Revelation 12:11). Your job is to testify that no weapon formed against you will prosper (Isaiah 54:17). Your job is to testify that the gates of hell don't prevail against you (Matthew 16:18).

We never have a right to murmur and complain. Jesus already warned us that *"in the world [we] will have tribulation"* (John 16:33 NKJV). We know that, so why complain about it? Why can't we just apply the answer to the problem? Life is about winning, and you win by doing things God's way and not your own way. Jesus said, *"Be of good cheer; I have overcome the world"* (v. 33).

At one time or another, everyone has been tempted to go another way and to do things contrary to God's Word. *"There is a way which seemeth right unto a man, but the end thereof are the ways of death"* (Proverbs 14:12). My friend, winning is doing it God's way.

We have to be steadfast when it comes to doing and saying it God's way. The Bible says,

> *Therefore, my beloved brethren, be ye stedfast, unmoveable, always abounding in the work of the Lord, forasmuch as ye know that your labour is not in vain in the Lord.*
> (1 Corinthians 15:58)

Holding fast to God's Word is not in vain. It will produce for you. I discovered this truth years ago, and I made up my mind to live according to

God's Word at all times. I decided I was going to speak God's Word in all situations.

Whenever I have become a little careless about saying what God said, my wife reminds me, "Wait a minute. That is not how I am used to hearing you talk." That gets me right back on track. There is a right way for Christians to live, and that way is by faith. (See Galatians 3:11.)

Faith calls those things that are not as though they were (Romans 4:17). Faith doesn't look at the things that are seen (2 Corinthians 4:18). If you walk by faith, you cannot walk by sight (2 Corinthians 5:7). You are to walk by the Word, not by your five physical senses.

So hold fast, especially when you're backed against the wall. Tell the Devil, "I am not going to stop speaking God's Word. You are not going to make me speak with a '*deceitful mouth*' or '*perverse lips*' (Proverbs 4:24 NKJV). I am going to speak words of life." This is a part of submitting yourself to God and resisting the Devil. And you know what? God said that the Devil will flee from you. (See James 4:7.) Expect it.

Change What Needs to Be Changed

Now the final thing you need to do to get your back off the wall is to change whatever needs to be changed. To accomplish this, you first have to accept the fact that sometimes change is needed. You cannot be married to certain methods and systems, because everything in our world is changing and progressing rapidly.

At one time, churches recorded their memberships by writing every member's name down on a roll, which was an enormous task. Today, most churches use computers. Television, computers, and other high-tech equipment are changing so fast that brand new products introduced this year are likely to be outdated by next year.

The Bible says that we change as Christians because we go *"from glory to glory"* (2 Corinthians 3:18). There ought to be change in our everyday lives. Sometimes, we have to change our methodology. We have to change our systems, our patterns, our ways, and even our means to an end. We can't afford to become so bonded to one idea, one strategy, or one method that we overlook God's attempts to show us new and better ways. He can open other doors and give us favor, revelation, and understanding that we never dreamed possible.

The four lepers who sat at the gate of Samaria, starving after the city was seized by the Syrians, said to one another, *"Why sit we here until we die?"* (2 Kings 7:3). What they were really saying was, "Let's change. Everyone in the city is already eating donkeys' heads and doves' dung, as well as human flesh. At least we are outside the gate and are free to leave. Our backs are against the wall. Why should we sit here doing nothing day in and day out until we die? Let us change what we can change. Let's try something different to make our situation better."

They did something different, the Bible tells us. They went to the Syrian camp to see if the enemy would take pity and feed them. Instead, they found the enemy had fled, frightened away by noises created supernaturally by God. The lepers found food and probably enough spoil to last them the rest of their lives. (See 2 Kings 7:1–20.)

Doing the same thing repeatedly could keep you from advancing. Why sit in the same place until you die? It does not make sense. There comes a point in all our lives when we need to change. You may need to change jobs, your conduct, your working hours, your disposition, your attitudes, or your perspective.

I grew up training to play professional tennis. My tennis coach would say things like, "This is how you should play this guy." "This one has a weak backhand." "That one's overhead stroke is weak." "He's not too swift on the court. Move him from side to side and get him to the net so that you can lob it over his head."

We would have it all mapped out. However, sometimes, I did exactly what the coach said on the court, yet I found myself losing. What encouraged me, though, was that my coach always ended his talks by saying, "If the plan doesn't work, change it."

In the church and business world, too many people stay with plans that no longer work. No game plan works forever. We must be able to adjust and make the appropriate changes.

Many people have sought personal assistance from our ministry over the years. Some we have helped joyfully, some reluctantly, and some we haven't been able to help at all. It was easy for us to help those who were tithing, committed, budgeting, and doing what they could in the natural to help themselves. They were in a spiritual position to be helped.

Others were con men looking for handouts. They felt sorry for themselves, but they didn't want to change anything. When we came across that kind of person, we would simply say, "Listen. We can't help you, because you need to change, and we don't see your willingness to change. We see that you have been doing the same thing for years—living off other people—and you are not going to live off us. You need to change."

Some of you may have a nice job that pays good money, but you have to travel long distances to get to work and back home. You don't have enough time with your family, and your car is always in the shop. Your situation might call for a change, because you really are not getting ahead. Sometimes, to get ahead, you have to change.

Changing may also mean going back to school. It might mean leaving your present job, even if you have been there ten or twelve years. If you are working for retirement benefits or a pension, but missing all of the important things in life as you go, those retirement years will be bittersweet when they finally come. It never pays to mark time, simply letting today pass by to get to tomorrow. Change your job and lifestyle so that you can enjoy life and be used by God now.

A change in your marriage may be necessary. I'm *not* talking about changing spouses, but changing your attitudes and behavior toward the one you have.

Sometimes, I hear people say, "My husband (or my wife) has changed." Depending on the circumstances, it may be good that their spouses have changed. If the changes are good and positive, then you should be glad about it. We are supposed to change.

The Only Constant in Life Is Change

You are changing anyway, whether you want to or not. Your environment is changing you. The people around you are changing you. You are changing because of age and because of experiences. You are changing all the time. Good or bad, you are changing.

In relationships, there are times when one partner changes for the better and the other one feels threatened and left out. Often, what we're really saying is we still like to compromise, but our spouses don't. Perhaps the wife has outgrown her husband spiritually and no longer enjoys watching all the junk on television as she grows stronger in the Lord. She doesn't drink beer now because she's growing spiritually. Maybe she doesn't want to attend any more social events where there is drinking, cursing, and other ungodly behavior. Yet her husband says, "She's changed" and describes her as "not being any fun."

I would ask those husbands, "Well, what happened to your relationship with Jesus? If your relationship with Jesus was right, then you would not want to go to those places or watch those shows either. And you and your wife could change and grow together."

We are supposed to grow in the things of God and get better, aren't we? A change supposedly takes place in every Christian, but that can cause problems in the home if both the husband and the wife aren't interested in growing spiritually.

You want to grow and change in the things of God. If you purpose in your heart to do so, here are some of the things you might have to change:

- Your view about what builds your self-esteem (pleasing God or pleasing others)
- Your image, your attitudes, and your perspective on life
- The way you budget your money or the way you view it
- Your job or career (going back to school, taking technical courses, relocating, etc.)
- Your church, if you are not in a place where the full Gospel is being taught and practiced
- Your friends, if they are a hindrance to your growth in God
- What you watch on television (videos and movies you see)
- The books and magazines you read
- The places you go for entertainment or relaxation

When you're backed against the wall, my friend, one of the first things you ought to do is compare your hours spent watching television with the hours you spend reading or hearing the Word of God. Then change your habits, because obviously, the television has not helped you.

Acts 18:24–28 gives an account of a man named Apollos, who changed for the Lord's sake. He was *"an eloquent man, and mighty in the scriptures"* (v. 24). He was *"fervent in the spirit"* (v. 25). He spoke and taught diligently about spiritual things (v. 25), but he had been instructed in the way of the Lord up to a certain point.

He began to speak boldly in the synagogue and

> *when Aquila and Priscilla had heard, they took him unto them, and expounded unto him the way of God more perfectly. And when he was disposed to pass into Achaia, the brethren wrote, exhorting the disciples to receive him: who, when he was come, helped them much which had believed through grace: for he mightily convinced the Jews, and that publicly, showing by the scriptures that Jesus was Christ.* (Acts 18:26–28)

When Aquila and Priscilla heard how Apollos was articulate, diligent, and mighty in the Word, and they saw his sincerity, they took him under their wings and *"expounded"* (v. 26) or explained to him the way of God more completely. Evidently, he recognized and accepted the fact that a change was needed, and upon doing so, he was able to strongly convince the Jews in Achaia that Jesus was the Christ.

My point here is that Apollos changed! Although he was mighty in Scripture, eloquent and fervent, he changed. Apparently, he was a great orator, but he still needed to change, and he did so. He was willing to change and was teachable.

He was open to learning more about God. You have to stay teachable at all times because new methods and new ideas come to us frequently. You can't stay married to one game plan and one method for the rest of your life.

Many people misunderstood Oral Roberts when he stopped going around the country preaching to people in tents. He said, "God is speaking to me about television. I can reach more people through television than I can through holding tent meetings around the nation." He changed, because times were changing.

Today when you talk to business people by telephone in different states and foreign countries, one of the first things they ask is if you have a fax machine or E-mail. "We'll fax it to you," they say. Nowadays, you can bypass the one-, two-, and three-day wait by faxing.

But the key is that you must be open to change. You have to change methods, systems, and ideas to better yourself. Too many of us have routines etched in stone that we are not willing to alter or compromise; consequently, the world is leaving us behind. I'm not going to live in the Stone Age. I'm going to change when I need to change to improve my life and my existence. How about you?

When you're backed against the wall—

Change what needs to be changed.

Chapter 16

Fifteen Spiritual Exercises

In this book, there are fifteen points to help you get out of situations when you're backed against the wall. You may wonder if you should review this chapter and go over all fifteen points when you run into trouble.

Yes! Check to make sure that you are walking in these truths, remind yourself of each point, and do what you need to do. Make sure you are a doer of them and not just a hearer. Begin to apply them in your everyday life.

Point 1: **Guard your mind.**

Point 2: **Get specific instructions.** Get alone with God, shut your mind down, and see if God has anything to say about your particular situation. If He does, obey Him! If He does not, act out of a sound mind. Take control of your thoughts, and gird up your mind by the Word of God.

Point 3: **Be aggressive.** Don't retreat. Attack the situation, running toward your Goliath.

Point 4: **Remind God of His Word.**

Point 5: **Expect a miracle.**

Point 6: **Go to sleep.** Remind God of His Word, because He watches over His Word to perform it. You can expect a miracle because you have found out what God has to say about your situation. You don't have to worry about what the Devil is doing; therefore, you can go to sleep.

Point 7: **Don't count your life dear to yourself.** Don't fall in love with yourself. Don't compromise your relationship with God to save face and flesh. Face the situation, problem, mountain, or obstacle.

Point 8: **Evaluate the spirit in which you walk.** Will it be a lying spirit? Will it be a spirit of fear? Will it be a spirit of error or deception? Or will it be the Spirit of faith?

Point 9: **Remember who the Devil is, who you are, and who God is.** The Devil is a liar, you are a child of God, and God is almighty.

Point 10: **Give more for the work of God.** A Christian should always give tithes, regardless of what is going on in his or her life. Never take tithe money to pay bills—in good times or bad. Your tithe always goes to God. On the other hand, after you have given your tithe, you never take the money for paying bills and give it away. The Bible says, *"A good name is to be chosen rather than great riches"* (Proverbs 22:1 NKJV). Give your way out of trouble by eliminating unnecessary groceries, reducing the amount of gas you put in your car, or by cutting back on buying luxuries and incidentals. Also, you can give clothes, time, and food to someone who is sick or in need. Look for ways to give or to plant seeds.

Point 11: **Associate with winners.** Winners are the people you want to stay around. You do not want to be around a loser. You don't need to hang around someone who doesn't know where he's going or whether or not he can make it.

Point 12: **Fast and pray.** When you fast, seek God. Your purpose for cutting back on food is so that you can seek God's face and become more sensitive to your spirit.

Point 13: **Judge yourself.** (See 1 Corinthians 11:31.) Judge yourself to see if you are carrying unforgiveness, pride, or any other negative attitudes. The Bible says that we are to examine ourselves to see if we are in the faith. (See 2 Corinthians 13:5.) By judging yourself, you'll be able to see if you are walking in line with God's Word.

Point 14: **Praise and worship God.** Praise God by giving thanks to Him for what He has done. Worship God by showing love to Him for who He is. True praise and worship will bring deliverance.

Point 15: **Change what needs to be changed.**
Cling to your faith without wavering, no matter
what the situation looks like. Holding fast to God's
Word will produce for you every time. Then, finally, realize that you may need to change in order to move forward. We can't always do things
the same way—so stay open to change!

About the Author

Robyn Gool was born February 11, 1953, in Detroit, Michigan. At age nine, he received Jesus as his Savior. He also began traveling around the country playing tennis. In pursuit of a sports career, he accepted a tennis scholarship from Oral Roberts University. While at ORU, Robyn received the gift of the Holy Spirit and was called into Christian ministry in December 1972.

It was also at ORU that Pastor Gool met Marilyn, the young lady from Nassau, Bahamas, who was later to become his wife. From this union came three beautiful children: Robyn Johms, Marilyn Joi, and Sanchia Jentle.

In 1980 God led Robyn and Marilyn to begin an independent work in Charlotte, North Carolina. That work, Victory Christian Center, has grown in many ways since July 1980. At present, Sunday morning attendance runs over 2,000, and a full volunteer staff supports nursery, children's, and adult Bible classes. The outreach ministry, More than Conquerors Ministries, includes a daily television and radio program aired locally, a Bible school for laymen, and a school of ministry for those called into the ministry.

Pastor Gool has appeared on the Inspirational Network, Lester Sumrall's LESEA Alive telecast, and Richard Roberts Live. He has shared the Word of God both nationally and internationally for various ministries.

OTHER POWERFUL BOOKS
from Whitaker House

For Singles Only
Robyn Gool

This book contains timely advice for the Christian single in today's society. Preparatory tips for the physical, mental, financial, and spiritual facets of life are presented, as well as spiritual counsel for the unique problems and opportunities that face unmarried believers everywhere.

You should not begin dating, or go on another date, without reading this book!

ISBN: 0-88368-648-1   Trade   112 pages $6.99

Proper Attitudes toward Leadership
Robyn Gool

Attitudes can affect your success spiritually as well as naturally. A proper attitude can determine whether you win or lose. Robyn Gool explains how you should view leaders in the church and throughout your spiritual life. Discover the power and the blessing that accompany a positive attitude!

ISBN: 0-88368-650-3   Trade   160 pages $7.99